THE WINNING MIND

THE WINNING MIND

Fine tune your mind for
superior sports performance

PETER TERRY

THORSONS PUBLISHING GROUP

First published 1989

© Peter Terry 1989

Photographs reproduced courtesy of Allsport

British Library Cataloguing in Publication Data

Terry, Peter
The winning mind : fine tune your mind
for superior sports performance
1. Sports. Performance Psychological
aspects
I. Title
796'.01

ISBN 0-7225-1554-5

Published by Thorsons Publishing Group Limited,
Wellingborough, Northamptonshire, NN8 2RQ, England

Photoset by Rowland Phototypesetting Limited,
Bury St Edmunds, Suffolk

Printed and bound in Great Britain by
Woolnough Bookbinding Limited,
Irthlingborough, Northamptonshire

3   5   7   9   10   8   6   4   2

CONTENTS

DEDICATION

This book is dedicated with much love to my
Mother and Father and, of course, to Sue.

ACKNOWLEDGEMENTS

I gratefully acknowledge the contributions of:–
  Drs. Martin Lee and John White, for their invaluable feedback
  Sue Olliver, for her ideas and proof-reading
  John Brierley, for the impromptu seminars
  The students and athletes I work with, for their inspiration.

FOREWORD BY GERALD WILLIAMS

Author and television tennis commentator

When I was a young sports writer learning my craft in the North of England, I once spent a week near Hull working on a series of articles that the *Daily Mail* wanted me to write with Raich Carter. The probability is that I was so in awe to be drinking endless cups of tea in the kitchen of one of my boyhood heroes that many of his most priceless gems completely missed my attention.

This man, after all, played with Lawton and Matthews and Hagan in the England football team! Carter was all charisma, though we popular-papermen hadn't pinched the word from the theologians at the time.

All these years on, I remember above all one thing that Raich said. 'If I missed a scoring chance,' he snorted, 'I just couldn't wait to get the ball again in front of the goal. Then I'd stick it in the back of the net and say: 'There you are: sort that out!'

The point was, Raich Carter didn't fall apart when things went wrong. His confidence wasn't so flimsy that he immediately went into hiding. He knew he would score next time – and next time couldn't come quickly enough.

Some years later, when it seemed to have been decided that I was a tennis writer, I remember being in a small circle of players discussing together at the pre-Wimbledon tennis tournament at Beckenham. The Wightman Cup was also imminent, and we were talking about the breathless tension there is when matches like these are really close.

One of our group was a chatty, overweight, bespectacled little Californian on her first overseas trip and in the United States team for the match.

'Golly-gee!' ejaculated the American girl. 'Wow! Just imagine playing in the deciding rubber, and all the crowd going bananas. Gee, I just can't wait!' You've guessed it. She was Billie Jean Moffitt.

Again, no shrinking from the danger and the challenge but a bold, impatient welcoming of it.

What sets sporting champions apart from the journeymen? I am sure it is the mind. It is in their physical fitness, as well, as in their technique; and sometimes luck. But hoardes of also-rans are gifted athletes, stylish technicians.

If I had a pound for every person, in the last decade, who has asked me; 'When are you going to produce a British tennis champion?' I would have been able generously to supplement the considerable wealth that Wimbledon each year hands to the Lawn Tennis Association so that the LTA can revive our game. But Wimbledon knows that money can't produce champions: what it can do is create a system through which a champion can the easier emerge.

In British tennis, it seems to me, we now have a system at last. And Peter Terry is part of that system. Richard Lewis values greatly Peter's contribution to the development of Britain's best under-18 boys. And Richard Lewis is no admirer of cranks with crank panaceas. He is a stern realist.

Peter Terry is working very much on the minds of these boys. I doubt whether he can instil what is not innately there, but he can help develop that priceless, God-given virtue – the mind of a winner.

British sport has neglected that factor too long, so I welcome Peter Terry's contribution to the quest: both his work, one to one, with the youngsters, and now, through his book, to a far wider public.

Gerald Williams
1988

INTRODUCTION

This book has been written for those who play a sport and who wish to develop a winning mentality in themselves or in others. It is designed to equip you with the mental skills necessary to produce your best performances consistently, and it will help you whether you are a performer or a coach, whether you are an international athlete or just someone who wants to do a little better. Ask any champion athlete whether psychology is important in sport and the answer will always be the same – a resounding 'yes'. At the highest level it is often the crucial factor which separates the winners and the losers.

The mental side of performance will vary on a daily basis. If that weren't the case, then the most skilled tennis player would always win Wimbledon, the best golfer would triumph in the British Open year after year and Steve Davis would win every snooker tournament. As we all know, this doesn't happen. One of the joys of sport is that it is unpredictable, but at the same time this unpredictability can be a source of great frustration for all performers.

What are the typical excuses when you lose to an opponent you know you could have beaten? 'I just wasn't feeling right today,' 'I lost my concentration,' 'I wasn't aggressive enough,' or 'I talked myself out of that one.' And you always convince yourself that you'll get it right next time.

All these are valid and real reasons for poor performance, and all of them are within our powers of control. It is too simple to blame inconsistent performance on bad luck. It is usually due to poor psychological skills.

Most people do not fully understand how their mental approach affects their sports performance, and therefore they do not possess the mental skills needed to produce their best consistently. What this book is intended to do is to prepare you psychologically for competition, by explaining the mental side of sports performance. It is certainly not a magic wand, and it won't transform you overnight into a Boris Becker, a Steve Cram, or a Diego Maradona.

What it will do is help you concentrate better, help you improve your self-confidence, help you avoid 'choking' in crucial situations, and it will perhaps help you conquer that opponent who frustrates you so much. In short, the book will help to prepare you totally to be the best performer you are capable of being.

WHAT DETERMINES PERFORMANCE?

The first thing one must understand is that winning performances do not just happen. There is always a reason behind good and bad performances, and the first step towards a winning mentality is an examination of how performance is controlled. Therefore, the introductory section of this book analyses sports performance and explains its component parts. It then discusses each element of performance in turn, to help you build a clear picture of your strengths and weaknesses as a competitor.

Stated simply, your performance in any sport will be determined by a combination of three things. These are: your *skill level*, your *physical preparation* for the competition and your *psychological readiness* to compete.

The relative importance of these factors will differ from sport to sport. For instance, racing cyclists rely heavily on physical conditioning but devote little time to the actual skill of pedalling, while top golfers, who need constant practice to keep their skills razor sharp, can perform well with relatively low levels of aerobic fitness. Similarly, developing stamina is much more important for a marathon runner than for someone who plays darts, a sport described by one journalist as 'the pot-bellied performing for the gratification of the pea-brained'. Darts, on the other hand, involves very precise skills which require more practice than the relatively straightforward and repetitive skill of running efficiently.

However, the element of performance that makes demands of all sports people equally is the psychological readiness to compete. Without mental toughness no athlete can be considered fully armed for competition. And yet most people enter the sports arena having given no thought to mental preparation. If even a tiny fraction of the time you spend on fitness work and skills training were to be devoted to improving your mental approach to sport you would at least be giving yourself the chance to avoid the frustrations of inconsistency.

This book explains how performance in sport is affected by your mental attitude, both to your opponent and to your sport, and it includes a programme of psychological preparation which you should learn and practise. All you need to do is to acknowledge the importance of mental toughness, and to dedicate sufficient time and effort to allow your mental skills to develop in harmony with your physical skills.

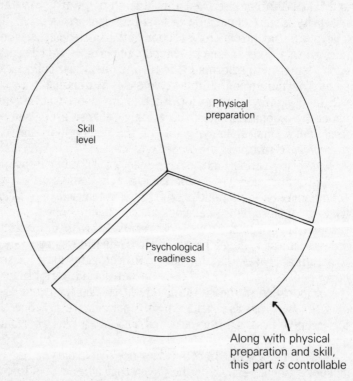

Performance = Skill level + Physical preparation + Psychological readiness

Skill level

Physical preparation

Psychological readiness

Along with physical preparation and skill, this part *is* controllable

If you want the whole pie make sure *you* complete the formula

Fig 1.1

**If you want to win,
prepare mentally as well
as physically**

THE THREE COMPONENTS OF PERFORMANCE

Skill

A clear view of this component of performance is clouded by the proliferation of terms, such as 'ability', 'talent' and 'technique', which all relate to proficiency in sport. The term *skill* refers to the capacity to produce a desired result consistently and with efficiency of time and effort. Despite what appearances, myth and sports journalists may sometimes suggest, skill in sport is not simply a gift from God. Athletes do not inherit skills, they acquire them. Skill is invariably the result of endless hours of personal sacrifice and practice. Not even Seve Ballesteros emerged from the womb skilfully swinging a nine iron. Until he had mastered the simple skill of walking and the knack of hand-eye co-ordination he was unprepared to even attempt his mastery of golf.

But how do we explain the skills of Diego Maradona or Steffi Graf, whose genius places them head and shoulders above their fellow soccer and tennis professionals? Perhaps in the final analysis the rare gifts of the sporting virtuoso defy even the most rigorous scientific scrutiny, but, in theory at least, they are nothing more complicated than supreme examples of *ability trained to perfection*. But if we explore the theory further, perhaps we can highlight the nature of ability and training. Unarguably, basic *ability* underlies superior performance. Equally, it could be said that skill also underlies performance, but do not confuse the two terms.

Sporting ability will often emerge very early in life, in the form of general abilities such as good balance, co-ordination, intelligence, a sharp eye, or a retentive memory. These qualities will equip one for many sports because they act as the foundations upon which skills are built. Intelligence is required to understand skills, memory is required to retain them once learnt, balance, co-ordination and good eyesight will all aid performance. Skill training, which involves moulding and refining ability for a specific activity, is certainly easier when these qualities are present, but natural ability is by no means essential for producing a competent athlete.

How does skill develop?

Skill development involves understanding the relationship between what we want to achieve and the physical responses that are required to bring it about. Note that skill is about understanding that relationship and not necessarily about having the physical and psychological qualities to make things happen.

If you are learning how to throw a ball, for instance, you soon come to realize that by varying the position of your body, the angle at which the ball is released, and the force that you apply to the throw, you can vary the speed, distance and direction the ball travels. The way you learn is by comparing what you wanted to happen with what actually happened after each throw. Your senses play a vital role in this process. Sight tells you whether the ball did what you wanted it to do. Your sense of touch tells you how the action felt, and gradually you learn to distinguish between what felt right and what felt wrong. If you identify the errors correctly – and here you often need the experienced eye of a coach or teacher to help you – your next attempt can be modified accordingly. The more balls you throw, the better you will understand the relationship and therefore the more skilful at throwing you become.

Eventually you become very good at pre-setting the correct position of the body, and the angle and force of release for the required distance, and you also become much more sensitive to the errors in your performance. This understanding is stored in your memory like a computer program, ready to be called upon whenever you need to throw something. In a similar fashion, programs are developed for the basic sports skills of running, jumping, catching and kicking, as well as throwing.

Psychologists disagree about the age at which these programs are developed. Some argue that the seeds for all future sports skills are sown in the first two years of life, while others feel that the period between the ages of 7 and 13 is the critical time. Most experts, however, would agree that these skill programs are developed during childhood and moulded later. Some children develop their basic skills so thoroughly that they appear to pick up more complex sports skills in later life without really trying. These so-called natural athletes reap the benefits as adults of childhoods spent experimenting with a wide range of sporting activities and equipment.

Evidence suggests that experimentation is probably more important than coaching at an early age. This is because almost as much can be learnt about how to achieve certain outcomes by producing them incorrectly as by continually repeating a correct, prescribed movement. Trial and error is an effective way of learning sports skills because it helps develop a feel for right and wrong. Although adults will tend to be guided quite rigidly by coaches towards correct technique, a complete lack of experimentation with movement carries the risk of producing stereotyped, robotic, and therefore predictable performers. Introducing flair and versatility into your game requires some variability in your practices, so do not be afraid to practise what is unconventional.

Another unfortunate tendency, even among highly competent athletes, is to practise those skills at which they are already very good, rather than spending time on those areas where they are deficient. This is particularly evident in group activities and is explained primarily by the ego defence systems which are well developed in most people. We all try to avoid embarrassment, and nobody wants an audience to witness poorly executed or ungainly movements, so when others are watching we prefer to fall back on the old faithfuls in our sporting repertoire. The long-term effect of this tendency is to widen the skills gap between our strong points and our weaknesses.

Even some of the all-time greats had potentially serious flaws in their game. The brilliant Welsh scrum half Gareth Edwards never mastered the spin pass off his left hand, while the England soccer star Norman Hunter rarely used his right foot for anything other than standing on. These stars reached the top despite their limitations, but most people need a comprehensive range of skills to ensure success. Sporting opponents will eventually identify the weaknesses in your game and exploit them. A winning mentality requires you to get there first, by identifying the weak links in your own skills chain and working hard to strengthen them, and also by spotting your opponent's weakness and attacking it ruthlessly.

How well are sports skills retained?

Compared to other types of skills, such as knowledge of a foreign language, sports skills are quite durable, once the movement programs are developed. Even with the minimum of practice a reasonable level of proficiency can be maintained, particularly in those who have mastered their craft. That is not to say that sports skills will stick around unused for ever. Soccer genius George Best once said, 'Skill is something I'll never lose. I'll have that when I'm 100.' There is an element of truth in this statement, but there is also a large degree of self-delusion, or perhaps just wishful thinking.

Because skill involves understanding *how* to achieve certain results, in theory one should be able to retain it indefinitely. However, there are factors which make it unlikely that the ability to translate skill into performance will last forever. For a start, ageing takes its toll upon our physical functioning: joints stiffen and muscle fibres deteriorate. Eminent physiologists have estimated that about 50 per cent of the decline in our performance with advancing years is due to the effects of the ageing process. For the most part this is beyond our control. However, the remaining 50 per cent can be largely explained by the fact that we may no longer be utilizing our talents. In fact, ageing and disuse of our talents conspire to form a vicious circle, so that as we grow older we increasingly lack the confidence to use our physical capabilities, which diminish as a result, which in turn further decreases our confidence to use them. In other words, if you fail to *use* your skills and physical abilities, then in time you will *lose* your strength, or your stamina, your agility, your golf swing, or your tennis serve, or any of the wide range of physical skills you may have had. In effect, skills will be gradually forgotten by the body unless used.

As you have probably noticed, this applies to some skills more than others. The old saying that 'you never forget how to ride a bicycle' is usually true and could apply equally well to swimming. These are relatively simple, repetitive skills involving whole limb movements where accuracy of movement is less important than continuity of action. With more refined skills involving the manipulation of an implement such as a dart, a snooker cue, a racquet, or a ball, you can become rusty in a very short space of time. Although the skills never entirely desert you, timing is lost and skill patterns become blurred. So although we are limited in the extent to which we can counter the effects of ageing, we have direct control over preventing the decline due to disuse. What you need to recognize is that skills rely upon practice for their preservation as well as their development. So the message is clear:

> # Practice is vital in maintaining skills. Use them or lose them!

Practice schedules

Really effective practices need to be carefully thought out to suit the needs of the individual. Frequency of practice, duration of practice, intensity of practice, and type of practice are all important variables in skill development and skill maintenance. The thinking athlete frequently questions his or her own practice schedules. The acid test for any type of practice should be whether performance is being enhanced. If not, there may be something wrong.

Be mindful that the old adage 'practice makes perfect' is not strictly true. For a start most sportspeople would deny the existence of the perfect performance. World records are always broken eventually, so the most we can hope for is to be the best at any particular time, or to be better than we once were. Also, while practice is certainly the most important variable in the skill development process, inappropriate practice is almost as bad as no practice. Similarly, practice in the absence of a reliable source of accurate feedback will result in little or no learning, because poor technique may be practised over and over again.

A more reasonable equation might be 'appropriate practice with appropriate feedback makes better' and while this is a terrible mouthful, the modifications are important. You may well be asking the question, 'What is *appropriate practice* and *appropriate feedback*?' There is no simple answer to either part of the question, but as far as practice is concerned you might consider the following recommendations when you design your practice schedules, or even if you rely on a coach for advice:

- Skills which cannot be mastered in their complete form need to be broken down into their component parts, practised separately, and gradually pieced together again. But beware of dissecting skills so far that the overall aim of the movement is lost entirely

- Do not sacrifice quality for the sake of quantity. If you become exhausted during practice you will end up just going through the motions. Allowing yourself adequate recovery periods during a session gives time to digest feedback from the previous activity period and enhances learning

- Remember that practices should always be realistic, to ensure the skills that develop carry over to contest situations. If, for instance, you play a sport where opponents play closely against each other, such as hockey, basketball, or soccer, and you only practice your skills unopposed, you may find that they deteriorate when opposition is introduced. The additional time and space available can foster movement patterns which won't be effective in the real game. Un-opposed practices are useful in the early stages of developing a skill but realism needs to be introduced at some stage

- Consider the emphasis you are placing upon speed of movement and accuracy of movement in practice. Generally speaking, you sacrifice some accuracy of movement as you increase speed of movement, but for all skills there is an optimum combination of the two. This speed–accuracy trade-off is evident with players who take soccer penalty kicks: some prefer to sacrifice the speed of their shot for an accurate placement of the ball, while others prefer to blast the ball towards the goal, and don't aim it at any spot in particular. Once you have analysed the speed–accuracy requirements of your skills you should practice accordingly

- There is conclusive research to prove that practising skills mentally as well as physically can offer a significant improvement in performance compared to physical practice alone. Many people will run through performances in their mind before or after a contest, but the most effective results come from adopting a systematic approach to mental practice. Many of sport's great practitioners are adept at practising mentally. The principles of this strategy are explained in Chapter 7.

The question of appropriate feedback is also crucial to skill development. In the sporting context, feedback can be viewed as any information relating to skilled movement which may change future movement patterns, confirm the correctness of current ones, or motivate an individual to continue.

Feedback is your constant companion during performance. As you perform any skill, your senses are bombarded with information regarding the nature of that performance. If you are a tennis player, for example, feedback is available with each shot. You can see where the ball lands, you can hear the sound of the ball on the racquet, and you can sense the feel of the shot by the sensations through your wrist, arm and shoulder. Notice that it is not only what you see and what you hear that aids learning; all your senses contribute to the process, and your internal sense of feel (sometimes known as proprioception) plays a particularly vital role.

Sportspeople talk a lot about getting the 'feel' for a sport. This implies that performance is dependent upon the information relayed back and forth between your limbs and your brain. Interpreting this information accurately forms a large part of skill learning. When you perform any skill for the first time, particularly one involving unfamiliar body positions, it will feel strange and, where rotation of the body through more than one axis is involved, as in a complicated trampolining move, it is often completely disorientating. Quite simply, you will not understand the sensations your body is providing for you, partly because they are unfamiliar to you and partly because they are too numerous and too fast for your brain to process effectively.

With repetition comes familiarity and, eventually, an understanding of those feelings which are important and those which can be ignored. But during the early stages of the learning process this information overload can mean that the novice is completely unaware of important information related to performance. The novice golfer, for instance, will typically lift his head before the shot is completed, often quite unconsciously, because of a reflex which links head and shoulder movement. A learner with this problem would possibly benefit from an observer pointing out the fault, but it is far from certain. Because novices require time and all their concentration to sort the useful from the irrelevant feedback, that observer may actually be making a hard job more difficult. In fact, research suggests that complete beginners may benefit most from a clear demonstration and then a period of uninterrupted practice to allow them a feel for the movement before they receive coaching.

Experienced players have a different problem as far as feedback is concerned. After repeating a movement many times, much of the feedback received from the body becomes redundant and is ignored unless it feels very different. The movement will continue to feel correct unless it varies significantly. The problem here is that gradual changes to technique can occur undetected, allowing major faults to develop unnoticed. Although frequent sliced or hooked shots make it obvious to a golfer that a fault exists, identifying the exact cause may be extremely difficult if it continues to feel like a normal swing. This is where additional feedback from a good coach or a video may be necessary.

For expert performers this problem can be even more acute. Because they have little need to think about the mechanics of producing certain movements, they devote their concentration almost exclusively to tactical considerations. When little attention is paid to technique, minor changes can become deeply ingrained over time and prove very difficult to eradicate. Professional golfers, for instance, who develop subtle errors in their game often talk of 'taking their swing apart'. This means that they return to the very basics and relearn them, slowly piecing together their former skills, ironing out the faults as they go. Such a process can be a painfully slow and depressing business.

The moral here is to pay close attention to technique, whatever your performance level, in order to correct minor faults before they become a real problem. If possible, seek regular advice about your technique from an expert coach to ensure that the feedback you receive is accurate. Remember that fellow athletes will freely offer you advice about your technique. They can always see exactly what you are doing wrong, or so they think, and they are not slow to give you a complete list of your impediments. Coaching sports skills is a very complex job and often a little knowledge is a dangerous thing. Casual advice from fellow competitors may turn out to be right or it may prove to be wrong, but be aware that a sure way to have your performance destroyed is to be told of half a dozen errors in your technique and to attempt to correct them all at the same time. Humans are not capable of processing large amounts of information simultaneously. Good coaches work on one fault at a time. They identify errors accurately and they devise practices to correct them. So, if your technique is letting you down seek the advice of the most knowledgeable and experienced coach you can find. A winning mentality includes knowing where to find the expertise to tune your skills to the ideal pitch.

Here is a recipe carefully devised to give you the best chance of perfect results.

Sports skills

(Serves one)

Ingredients: Ability
Practice
Feedback

1 Take a generous measure of sporting ability.
(NB The average person contains more than enough for most sports purposes.) Be careful not to underestimate your own potential. Thoughtful handling will greatly enhance the flavour.

2 Arrange sufficient practice.
This may take anything from hours to years depending upon your requirements, but remember, quality is more important than quantity.

3 Add feedback as necessary.
This vital ingredient is sometimes difficult to obtain, so consult an expert. Avoid inferior or excess feedback, either of which may impair your progress.

Once your skills have matured, combine them with prime fitness and the toughest sporting mentality you can obtain. Display in a bowl (the superbowl perhaps!) or any sporting arena.
   Serve with relish.

Does skill guarantee performance?

Does a high skill level ensure good performance? It may seem that the answer is yes, but on its own skill is not enough. It is very important to emphasize the gap between skill level and performance level. One represents potential, the other represents production. Skill is rather elusive and is intangible. You cannot see it or touch it. All you can see is *skilled performance*, the manifestation of potential, and it is worth remembering that your performance, although undoubtedly the best indicator of skill level, is a far from perfect measure of how much skill you have within you.

Consider the skills of Glenn Hoddle. If he pulls a muscle or twists an ankle you could hardly expect him to produce a great performance. But has he lost his skill? Has it evaporated in an instant? Absolutely not! The skill remains but the ability to perform has been temporarily impaired. Providing no permanent damage has been done, the skills will flow again when the injury mends.

It is usually apparent when physical defects are causing poor performance, but when the problem is one of mental approach it may not be obvious. As the saying goes, 'there's many a slip 'twixt cup and lip', and often the processes required to enable skill to be translated into the type of performance you are truly capable of fail to stand up to the pressures of competition. You may often be left frustrated by the discrepancy between what you are capable of producing, or even regularly produce in practice, and what sometimes emerges during an important contest.

Sport has a long history of favourites who failed in major competitions. Track and field athletics has produced more than its share of world record holders who then succumbed to 'lesser' opponents in Olympic finals. The 10,000 metre runners Ron Clarke of Australia and the British athlete Dave Bedford are spectacular examples of this. Even the fantastic achievements of Sebastian Coe were marred for nearly a decade because he wasn't able to win a gold medal for the 800 metres in a major championship. Coe did ultimately win the gold medal for this event in the 1986 European championships. Eventually, his actual performances matched those of which everyone knew he was capable, but which for some reason had deserted him during crucial races.

When the discrepancy between potential and performance is displayed so obviously by the world's greatest athletes it is not difficult to appreciate that the problem must affect us all.

Fitness

What is fitness?
Fitness is often mistakenly assumed to be something you either possess or you do not. People tend to be viewed in black or white

terms, applauded as 'fit' or dismissed casually as 'unfit', as though it were tattooed across their forehead. Fitness is not a difficult concept to understand but neither is it simplistic enough to be viewed in this way.

Fitness is first and foremost a relative term which refers to the ability of the body to perform work. Everybody is capable of some work unless they are completely infirm, and therefore everyone has some level of fitness. However, the level of work you are capable of producing is related to the level of work you usually produce. For example, the middle aged man who jogs regularly will find running considerably easier than a colleague of the same age who never runs. This is obvious, but why does it occur? It occurs because fitness is based on the *overload principle* which determines that the capacity to respond improves only when the demand placed upon an organism – such as your body – increases. Therefore, as you gradually increase the amount of work you usually demand of your body, you correspondingly increase the ability of your body to perform higher levels of work. That is, your fitness will depend upon how much, how often and how vigorously you exercise.

With increased exercise the body will adapt to a new reality and will become fitter. Even brisk walking, gentle jogging or swimming will make you fitter if they exceed your present activity level. Whatever your current level of fitness, if you start to exercise more regularly, for longer or with greater intensity, your capacity for work will grow. You are already on the road to improved fitness, so maybe you just need to step up a gear. There is no mystery to the principle that 'the more you do the more you are able to do', but naturally, the fitter you are already the harder it becomes to achieve further improvement. Proportionally, the greatest fitness gains can be made by those with low fitness levels.

Another important fitness concept is that of *specificity*, the tendency for training to improve performance in some activities whilst having a lesser effect, no effect, or even a detrimental effect, on the ability to perform other physical tasks. The popular view that a fit person should look a particular shape and be able to perform certain tasks is no more than a half truth. Consider the people on the next page. Which one is the fittest?

Zola Budd   Vasili Alexeyev

Carl Lewis   Olga Korbut

Question: 'Which one is the fittest?'
Answer: 'They all are!'

Well, in a way they all are! Zola Budd is the fittest for running distances, Carl Lewis is the fittest for sprinting, Vasili Alexeyev is the fittest for lifting weights, and Olga Korbut is the fittest for performing gymnastics.

Fitness is specific to the nature of the performance, and any conditioning work you undertake should be designed for the requirements of your sport. Broadly speaking, fitness can be considered to have four major elements: strength, speed, stamina, and suppleness – the four 's's of fitness. Most sporting events require some degree of all four but, referring back to our four superstars, distance running puts a premium on stamina, weightlifting requires great strength, sprinting clearly emphasizes speed, and suppleness is essential for all gymnasts.

When you are preparing yourself physically, think about which element of fitness you are trying to improve and how this is best achieved. As a guide:

- **Speed** is improved by repeating short periods of high intensity work, such as sprints or shuttle runs performed with adequate recovery periods.

- **Stamina** is improved through longer periods of low intensity exercise, such as steady running or swimming for a minimum of 15 minutes, but preferably 20 to 30 minutes.

- **Strength** is best developed using low repetitions of high resistance work, usually with weights.

- **Suppleness** is produced through regular stretching routines. Suppleness, or flexibility, is often referred to as the forgotten element of fitness but is necessary for most sports, particularly for preventing injury.

Two or three sessions per week are needed to significantly improve whichever element of fitness you are working on and it is feasible to combine more than one element into a single session. It is a good idea to do some suppleness work at the beginning and end of every session, and to try to complete sprint work before starting stamina work if you are doing both in a single session. Strength is probably best worked on separately, because it usually takes longest to recover from.

Generally speaking, one third of the time and effort spent acquiring fitness is required to maintain it. So if you did three sessions per week to gain strength you will need one session per week to keep it. One word of warning, though. It can be dangerous to plunge into a vigorous fitness programme that greatly exceeds the demands of your current lifestyle. Remember the following safety checklist:

- Start off your programme at a sensible level of exertion and build up slowly

- Always warm up and warm down with stretching exercises

- Use correct technique when lifting weights. Get advice from an expert at your local centre

- If you are in any doubt about your suitability for strenuous exercise, consult your doctor first.

These are only very basic guidelines for improving fitness; the high fitness levels required for outstanding performance involve specialized and highly specific training programmes. If you feel poor physical fitness is detracting from your performance and you are interested in specialist physical preparation for your particular sport there are many excellent books on the subject (see Further reading, p. 173).

Do everything you can to make fitness work enjoyable. Pleasant surroundings, pleasant company and realistic objectives will all aid your motivation. For a winning mentality you must have no doubts about your fitness. If you do, this will inevitably have a detrimental effect on your sporting confidence as a whole. Don't just play to get fit, get really fit to play!

The role of genetics

It is impossible to establish exactly what percentage of performance is determined genetically. Certainly factors such as height, build and muscle fibre composition predispose us towards some sporting activities rather than others. Ronnie Corbett, for instance, may be a reasonable golfer but he will never be a star basketball player. On the other hand, to talk of good genes and bad genes as the be all and end of all of future achievement is wrong.

The saying that you can't put in what God left out has some appeal, but sport is really more to do with trying to draw out what God *did* put in. There is great potential for performance within all of us, very little of which is ever realized. For example, physiologists acknowledge that only a small percentage of our potential strength is ever utilized at any one time. Rarely do more than 50 per cent of our muscle fibres 'fire off' during any voluntary muscle contraction, and that leaves a huge untapped reserve of strength. Exceptional circumstances sometimes allow us to reach in and harness these reserves. Women have been known to lift cars singlehandedly to save trapped babies. In sport, at the 1968 Mexico Olympic Games, Bob Beamon somehow summoned up enough power to long jump 29 feet, two-and-a-half inches, nearly 18 inches further than anyone had ever jumped before and further than anyone believed possible. Even 20 years later no one has been able to better this.

While it may not be possible to call upon these hidden reserves of strength at will, the simple acknowledgement of their existence should convince anyone that they are capable of performing far better than their present level of achievement. The four-minute mile was once an impossible dream, now the world's top runners are closer to three-and-a-half minutes. It is a disservice to mankind to talk of our absolute limits, and you will shackle yourself to mediocrity if you don't aim high and believe in yourself. In reality we may all be limited by genetics but the greater limitation comes from succumbing to the belief that we are limited. To scale new heights you must reach for the sky, and beyond.

Psychological readiness

The development of physical skills and fitness requires a systematic approach. A more efficient golf swing does not just materialize, strength gains do not simply happen. Top class athletes spend endless hours on relentless practice and physical toil in the justifiable belief that sports performance will be improved. But what of psychological preparation, and the mental toughness that sorts the winners from the also rans?

Athletes may accept concentration lapses, loss of motivation, and a sudden plunge in performance (which is referred to as 'choking') with resignation, although they would never resign themselves to poor fitness or a weak backhand. Too often, psychological readiness is the random factor in performance, seen as part of sport's rich tapestry. This is a fundamental misconception. Psychological preparation for sport is not only possible, it is relatively easy to achieve with suitable guidance and sufficient dedication. The purpose of learning psychological skills is to bridge gaps between athletic potential and performance. Nobody performs to the best of their ability during every sporting contest. Sometimes this may be explained by variations in physical conditioning, but usually it is due to fluctuations in our mental state. Confidence, anxiety, motivation, and concentration are all vital components of performance. They have a profound influence on the extent to which performance reflects potential. If you control them you control performance. This is explained in Fig. 1.2.

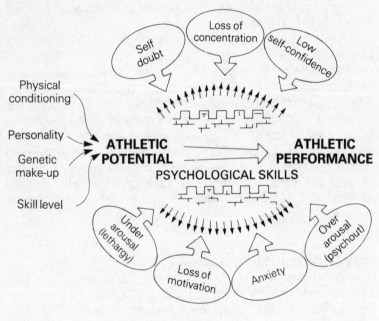

Fig. 1.2

The hours spent on physical conditioning and skill development, coupled with genetic characteristics and aspects of personality, endow all athletes with their own potential for sporting achievement. Whether they are able to translate this potential into a corresponding level of performance depends upon their resistance to disruptive forces. If you are mentally tough you perform at a level near that of which you are capable. If your psychological skills are poor you may rarely or never reach these performance levels. Anxiety, self-doubt, poor concentration, loss of motivation, and low self-confidence – these are the enemies within. Collectively they can diminish your performance until it is a shadow of its true potential. Building a tough mental approach to your sport is the way to keep these problems at bay. Mental toughness allows your performance to truly reflect your potential. It is not any easier to develop psychological skills for sport than it is to develop physical skills and fitness, but neither is it any more difficult. If sport is important and you are determined to be a winner, mental toughness is essential to your game.

GETTING MOTIVATED, STAYING MOTIVATED

Sportspeople the world over talk a lot about motivation. They say it is important, and they are right. They say some people are more highly motivated than others, and again they are correct. Many of them believe that if you are not motivated for a particular activity or a specific sporting occasion, then there is nothing you can do about it. But this is not true. Although great self-motivation is a characteristic of many champions, motivation can be consciously manipulated. Anyone who has noticed how their own motivation fluctuates with the seasons or is dependent simply upon their mood, should appreciate that by understanding themselves and the principles of motivation they can influence not only their willingness to participate, but their determination to persist and their resolve to try harder as well.

The term motivation comes from the Latin word 'movere' meaning to move and describes the force within us which activates us to direct behaviour in a certain way. We often refer to this force by other names. Sometimes, when the spirit prevails against great adversity, we call it 'guts', for example, when marathon runner Jim Peters, with his body on the very edge of physical collapse, tottered and crawled to the finishing line in the 1954 Empire Games. We might use the term 'drive' to describe the force by which Edwin Moses, for instance, keeps pushing himself to victory after victory when he has already beaten the world's best many times over.

Whatever we choose to call it, motivation is clearly an important component of performance, and without it we are never psychologically ready to compete. Its impact is fundamental even to our daily lives. A complete absence of motivation would mean inertia, no activity at all. This is a totally unnatural state for the

Motivation – Boris Becker

human species, as we all possess a deep-rooted need to explore and master our environment. Therefore, nobody is entirely devoid of motivation. What you may need to discover is the key which unlocks your own motivational reserves.

We must start by understanding how motivation is activated. Remember that at any moment we may be faced with a dilemma. Life, with its infinite variety, offers us a vast range of activities which compete for our time. If offered a choice, some people would choose to go for a walk, some would play sport, some would lounge around, and some would choose to read a book, as you are now. One person may tire of their chosen activity quickly and decide to stop, whereas another may persist much longer. Likewise, one person may devote only part of their energy to the task at hand while another may dedicate every ounce of vigour to the activity.

These differences illustrate the three dimensions of motivation:

- Selectivity – referring to the tendency to pursue one particular activity in preference to any other

- Persistence – referring to the tendency to continue an activity until a particular aim is fulfilled

- Intensity – referring to the amount of energy devoted to the activity.

So, while one person may demonstrate a very intense attitude towards sport and persist doggedly until they achieve success, a second individual may participate only half-heartedly, and settle for something easier if the going gets tough.

HOW PERSONALITY INFLUENCES MOTIVATION

There are two aspects of personality which particularly affect motivation in competitive situations. They are usually referred to by the terms *need for achievement* (NA) and *fear of failure* (FF). NA refers to the degree to which each one of us is naturally competitive and actively seeks out the sort of challenge which

How the need for achievement and fear of failure influence motivation for competition

Type 1

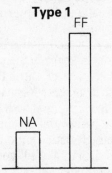

Type 2

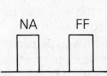

This person will often leave jobs unfinished or lose interest in activities. They will avoid competition if possible but might compete against someone they know they will beat, such as playing tennis against the neighbour's six-year-old son.

This person feels indifferent towards competition and would probably wonder why people make such a fuss about winning and losing. 'After all, it's only a game,' they might say.

Type 3

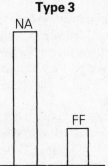

Type 4

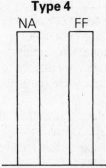

This person loves competition, especially where the outcome is uncertain. They are full of energy towards a particular goal, they take calculated risks, they love to win but realize that losing is not the end of the world. They are very persistent and highly self-motivated. These are ideal characteristics for a champion athlete.

This person also enjoys competitive situations and takes personal responsibility for outcomes, but failure causes self-doubt and lower self-esteem. This inner conflict often emerges in the form of poor sportsmanship, an unwillingness to take risks, decreased persistence, and even psychosomatic illnesses. As a result of these traits many sportspeople fail to fulfil their potential.

Fig 2.1

sport provides. FF refers to the way we view the possibility of defeat. Although no sportsperson enjoys losing, defeat is more damaging for some than for others. There are many for whom failure results in self-doubt and low self-esteem, and this inevitably has a detrimental effect on motivation.

NA and FF are independent personality characteristics, which means that an individual may be high in one and low in the other, high in both or low in both. To understand yourself a little better see how you compare to the descriptions in fig. 2.1. As an active sportsperson, you may feel you have little in common with types one and two. Sport, after all, is highly achievement-orientated. However, if you *do* recognize these characteristics in yourself, your commitment to winning will be less than total. Ask yourself *why* sport attracts you and what you hope to get out of it. Many sportspeople have reasons for participating which do not revolve around achievement but are related to friendships, personal respect and the exhilaration of movement. There is nothing wrong with this. If your need for achievement is low, recognize it, accept it and enjoy participation for reasons other than winning in the conventional sense. Anyone who is happy in their sport is a winner in my book.

If you see yourself as type three, then motivation for competition will not be a major problem for you. However, you may not find training challenging enough, and therefore effective goal setting, which is explained later in this chapter, may be necessary to maintain your natural motivation through the long hours of practice.

Type four individuals are very common in sport. Often they have all the talent and will have excelled in sport as youngsters, when losing was virtually unknown to them. As a result, any failure becomes difficult to handle. Anxiety about losing, loss of motivation, and in some cases severe depression, can combine to cause under-achievement as adult athletes. Fear of failure causes many athletes to drop out because experiences in competition become too unpleasant. It is even possible to develop a *fear of success* which involves anxiety about the consequences of winning. More is expected of a champion: higher performance, further victories. The pressure of future demands and the exposure to public scrutiny can result in some athletes settling in just below the top level rather than really striving to be number one.

It is quite likely, of course, that you do not fit easily into any of

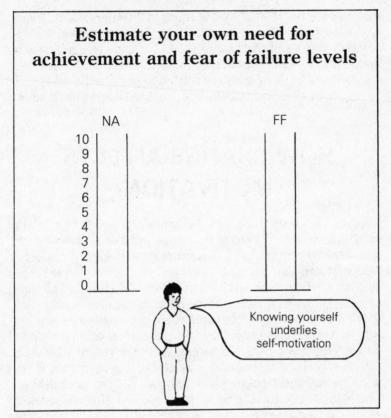

Exercise 1

the four categories. Perhaps your need for achievement and fear of failure levels are moderate. In this case you have much in common with millions of other normal, well-adjusted people, although by this I do not mean to imply, of course, that any of the four types described are maladjusted in any way.

Try to estimate your own NA and FF levels. Whatever view you take, a long, hard look at yourself will move you one step closer to the level of self-understanding which underlies improved motivation. You can then make changes if you do not like what you see.

You will need to accept that no adult is a piece of clay which can be moulded at will. To some extent, therefore, NA and FF are personal constraints within which you must learn to operate successfully. Equally though, no one is kiln-fired to the extent that they will resist small modifications to their personality. Even if, like leopards, we cannot completely change our spots, we are certainly capable of rearranging them. Begin by recognizing and bolstering the weak links in your motivational chain. Even if you decide that some problems *are* related to personality, many will be caused by situational factors which can be changed if you know how.

HOW CHANGE AFFECTS MOTIVATION

Everyone has heard the phrase 'a change is as good as a rest'. In reality the benefit of change lies in the fact that it creates new motivation. From research in industrial psychology, it has been demonstrated that the motivation and productivity of workers increases when their work environment is altered. This has become known as the Hawthorne effect and applies equally well to the sports environment. Often when professional sportsmen complain of becoming stale they take themselves off for a while to do something completely different, and then return with their batteries recharged, motivation restored, and are raring to go once again. Nigel Mansell plays golf, Ian Botham goes fishing. The high altitude training which has been so fashionable among international runners may well be beneficial as much in providing a fresh and stimulating training environment as for the physiological benefits.

Whereas Arsenal might wind down in the West Indies, or Liverpool might lounge around in Lagos, the likes of you and I will probably be forced to take more modest breaks in routine. This does not stop us from reaping the benefits of the change, though. Simple changes are often all that are necessary. Rugby players might try American football or Australian rules football, and so dispel those repetition blues which are so common during training. When the young tennis players at Bisham Abbey cease to fire on all cylinders an impromptu game of soccer usually restores their enthusiasm. The same principle applies to you as an individual. If training is getting you down or you are finding it difficult to stay really motivated, then try a temporary change of scene. It could turn out to be the breath of fresh air that gives you renewed impetus and vigour. Athletes too often become obsessive about their training routines, pursuing quantity at the expense of quality because they are afraid that a missed session will damage their programme. In fact, it is training which has become too arduous which can cause the damage. As a general rule, remember that overtraining can do more harm to performance than undertraining.

HOW YOUR ANALYSIS OF THE OUTCOME AFFECTS MOTIVATION

After any contest, we experience an immediate emotional response based on whether we win or lose. This can be anything from feeling 'over the moon' to feeling 'sick as a parrot'. It is natural for us to feel pleasure if we win and disappointment if we lose. However, we also experience a number of emotions such as satisfaction, guilt, pride, and depression, all of which depend not so much on the result of a contest but on our perceptions of *why* that outcome occurred. For instance, the underdog team who takes on and narrowly loses to First Division opponents in the FA Cup final would very likely be disappointed by the result but proud of their performance. The professionals of the First Division, on the other hand, would be relieved by the result but guilty about their poor showing. In the same way, any league squash player who gives it everything but loses against a player several divisions above him or her should feel a combination of disappointment and satisfaction.

Generally speaking, if people attribute their performance to things which they can control, such as their workrate, training and attitude, then pride or shame, satisfaction or dissatisfaction will be heightened one way or the other. If victory is believed to be due to a great effort, the result will be pride. If defeat is seen as the result of poor effort then a sense of shame will result. We defend our egos, so we tend to claim the credit when we win by attributing victory to our own effort and ability, but we like to shift the blame for defeat to things beyond our control such as bad luck, poor refereeing, adverse weather conditions and suchlike. The process of attributing causes to events is part of our need to make sense of the world in which we live, and the explanations we give ourselves affect not only our emotional reactions but our future motivation as well.

Do not allow yourself to believe that the outcome of a contest is beyond your control. Those people who believe that failure is an inevitable result of their poor ability typically react to losing situations with a shrug of the shoulders and a 'What's the point?' comment. This leads to lower levels of effort, reduced motivation and eventually these people will give up. To avoid feelings of helplessness and to foster the unshakeable belief in ability which characterizes the champion, learn to perceive failure as the result of some temporary factor. Such a factor might be poor form or bad luck, but a controllable variable like insufficient effort or incorrect training is more likely to motivate you to rectify the problem.

Believing yourself to be a success or a failure affects sports performance in many ways. Seeing yourself as a failure causes a loss of confidence, inhibits the way you play, and may even cause you to choose another, less depressing activity. On the other hand, seeing yourself as a success brings contentment, improved confidence, and the motivation to repeat the activity which brings about these feelings. Fortunately sport can provide enough success for everybody to get their fair share. Your perceptions of your own success belong to you and no one else. They are yours to use to your best advantage. The trick is to learn to recognize success.

The London marathon provides a classic example of success for all. Why would more than 20,000 people compete in a race that only one person can win, unless they each had their own criterion for success? Before any race, marathon runners set themselves many goals. Finishing the course, irrespective of the time it takes is usually one goal, and so it should be. A second goal may be to finish in a certain time, then perhaps the quality of the run may be important. 'Did it feel good?', 'Did I judge the pace well?' may be questions a runner will ask himself. The finishing position is almost irrelevant to all but the very élite runners. Individually and collectively, runners come away from the race feeling a sense of achievement. This is partly due to the feeling of communion with one's fellow man which any big event provides, as anyone who 'Ran the World' will testify, but the sense of achievement also comes from having fulfilled some or all of your predetermined objectives. Few people can run 26 miles and 385 yards and feel bad about themselves.

MOTIVATIONAL STRATEGIES

As you study the motivational strategies which follow, be aware that while all these techniques should help there is no single cure-all for low motivation. You should be prepared to give different strategies a try until you find the one which is right for you. Don't expect miracles. Try to find the acorn which one day may produce the mighty oak, and remember that learning how to use goal setting, personal contracts, or token rewards effectively is a skill you will need to work at like any other.

You may be one of those sportspeople who have as yet failed to realize the value of perseverance and hard graft. Sport is full of individuals who squander their talents by failing to apply themselves in training. Motivation can receive a significant boost just by acknowledging the absolute necessity for sustained effort. Looking back on the wilderness years before she broke through to superstardom, Martina Navratilova admitted, 'I didn't really train hard. Then I finally realized I couldn't just rely on what everyone called my natural abilities. I learned to work, and conscientiously and consistently to truly play at my capabilities.'

Clearly, success in sport eludes those who do not work for it. The world's greatest athlete, Daley Thompson, despite his supreme natural gifts, works harder than anybody, training many hours a day, day after day, week after week, year in, year out. Even if you cannot match his dedication, ask yourself whether your current level of effort in training really deserves the reward of winning performances. If you feel that it doesn't, then resolve to do something about it.

Admittedly, resolving to increase work and actually achieving it are two different things, but clearly that resolution is an important prerequisite. The point I am making here is that all the motivational strategies in the world will not help the person who has no real desire to be helped. *You* must decide what you really want to achieve in sport, then make a logical progression towards that goal.

SETTING GOALS

Setting goals is the process of defining clear objectives for yourself. It simply involves telling yourself what you intend to do and how well you intend to do it. This not only directs your attention towards a particular activity, but you also give yourself notice that a certain level of persistence and intensity of effort will be required. Whether consciously or subconsciously, you will almost certainly already be setting goals for yourself in many areas of daily life. If you make a simple plan of the day's activities or write out a list of jobs which need doing, you are setting goals. If you aim for international honours or set yourself the target of winning a particular contest, you are setting goals.

The whole concept of achievement is based entirely upon setting goals for yourself. If you fulfil your objectives you feel a sense of achievement. If you fall short of your objectives you feel a sense of failure. How clearly defined are your sporting goals? Your ultimate goals may have their roots in your childhood dreams of future glory. All boys have scored the winning goal at Wembley or the run which retained the Ashes at Lords. Perhaps nowadays it is more likely to be the touchdown which stole the Superbowl, or the final black to clinch the World Snooker Championship title. Such fantasies carry over into adulthood and become the foundation of ambition and self-belief. Even such vague goals, no matter how casually established, may set you on a specific path, but the all-important persistence and intensity with which you pursue objectives will depend not just on sustaining this dream but on the quality of your goal setting skills.

You should set goals for all aspects of your sporting life, from fitness work to skills training, from mental skills development to actual competitions, and even to your long-term career development. The well-known coach in track and field events, Wilf Paish, once said that all practices should be 'a competition . . . against yourself'. For maximum effort in training, set yourself objectives, try to beat your personal best performances whatever the exercise, be it bench presses, shuttle runs, or basketball free throws. Whatever your sport, get the best out of yourself by setting realistic but challenging targets every time you practice. Not only does this promote a sense of achievement but it provides a focus for each session. It can also demonstrate improvement which has not yet shown itself during competition performances, and equally importantly, it can make practice more fun.

Starting the process

At present the prospect of sitting down to mastermind your progress towards a far-off sporting triumph might daunt you. The list of sacrifices, the degree of effort, the range of skills to be mastered, can quite easily overwhelm you. Like the winning tape which seems to evade the 400 metre runner, so the path to your ultimate goal can appear to be an endless road which stretches out before you, riddled with potholes and barriers.

If this resembles your own situation, take heart from the wisdom of the Chinese. Confucius said that, 'Even the journey of a thousand miles begins with a single step.' Remember that the most unproductive time is spent worrying about all the things which need doing. You can only achieve one thing at a time, so learn to devote all your effort to the most immediate goal and forget about what lies beyond. For now your most immediate goal is to identify your destination. It may lie only a modest distance along the road of sporting achievement, or it may be a long and ambitious journey. Whatever you decide to aim for, the process is the same:

- Decide exactly what it is you wish to achieve

- Identify the obstacles that are preventing your progress

- Decide what is necessary to help you clear them

- Establish specific goals to help you tackle obstacles one by one.

Your certainty about your destination and the clarity with which you see the barriers will strengthen your determination to make progress.

Try completing exercise 2. At this stage it will only be the bare bones of a plan, just the first step forward. Think quite carefully about what you want to achieve. Aim for something which is a challenge but is within the bounds of possibility. Write it down in the 'Destination' box. Now express in your own terms the things you believe stand in your way. Write them down in the 'Barrier' boxes. Try to be specific but don't sweat over it for too long as you will be able to alter and refine your plan as you learn more about effective goal setting.

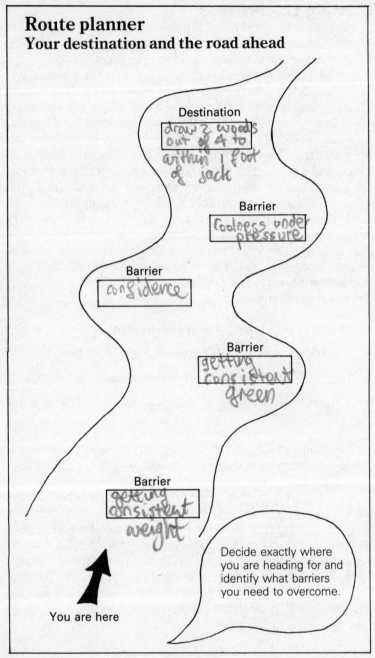

Route planner
Your destination and the road ahead

Destination

draw 2 woods out of 4 to within 1 foot of jack

Barrier

coolness under pressure

Barrier

confidence

Barrier

getting consistent green

Barrier

getting consistent weight

You are here

Decide exactly where you are heading for and identify what barriers you need to overcome.

Exercise 2

What sorts of goals will help you on your way?

Now that you have established the direction in which you are heading, you should start to consider specific objectives. The immediate temptation may be to establish goals in terms of winning contests. Obviously, winning is the ultimate objective, but too great an emphasis on this type of short-term goal risks damaging both motivation and confidence. Anyone with the solitary goal of winning a particular contest develops fixed attitudes about success and failure. Success is winning, losing is failure. This is a guarantee of failure at some stage because nobody can win all the time. People who have this attitude are being much too hard on themselves.

It is more constructive if the goals you set relate to things which contribute to winning but which you can directly control. These goals would include fitness, effort, aspects of technique, general strategies, and so on. These all allow for achievement, regardless of the result. Again I would say, 'Keep winning in perspective.' Always create for yourself a little piece of success that lies outside the result. Goals which are independent of the outcome of individual contests are an important means of maintaining motivation when the results may be going against you.

You will find that to set effective goals you must have a clear picture of your playing characteristics. For instance, if your sport is tennis you will need to assess each aspect of your performance on its own by assessing each skill in a systematic and detailed fashion. You must evaluate your serve, forehand groundstroke, backhand groundstroke, high volley, low volley, and so on. You will then need to do the same for each element of your fitness (speed, strength, stamina, suppleness), aspects of your mental approach (concentration, confidence, staying cool under pressure, etc.), and performance strategies (approaching the net, court position, etc.).

Using the example in exercise 3 as a guide, complete the exercise so that you can do a brief analysis of your own performance. If necessary, adapt the main headings to suit your particular sport. Avoid being too general with your comments; be as specific as you feel necessary. As the example indicates, you should use objective tests to assess performance wherever possible, but otherwise rate yourself out of ten. Eventually you will need to complete this exercise more thoroughly and you

Example of a completed performance analysis score sheet

Name: Colin Beecher   Age: 17

Sport: Tennis   Standard: Junior international

SKILLS	TEST	SCORE
* Serve	Point system	48
Smash	related to target	70
FH ground strokes	areas on court	68
* BH ground strokes	Percentage of	52
* High volley	maximum	44
Low volley	scored	59
Lob		72
Dropshot		64
FITNESS		
* Speed	Tennis court shuttles	9.8 (5)
Stamina	1 mile run	5min. 16 sec (9)
Strength	Bench press	76 kg (8)
* Suppleness	Sit and reach	+4 cm (3)
MENTAL APPROACH		
* Concentration	Scale 1-10	9
Coolness under pressure	"	4
Aggression	"	8
* Confidence	"	6
STRATEGIES		
Court position	Scale 1-10	8
* Approaching net	"	5
* Footwork	"	5
Shot selection	"	8

* Weaknesses

Performance analysis score sheet

Name: _____   Age: _____
Sport: _____   Standard: _____

SKILLS	TEST	SCORE
draw	Points system	
rest and lie	based upon	
1 foot behind	how often	
1 foot in front	a particular	
push up bowl	shot is	
1-2 foot short	bowled when	
trail jack	attempted	
firing		

FITNESS		
Stamina		
Suppleness		

MENTAL APPROACH		
Concentration		
Coolness under press		
Aggression		
Confidence		

STRATEGIES		
Shot selection		
Pacing game		

Exercise 3

would be well advised to seek help from your coach or someone
who knows you well as a player and as a person in order to assess
your performance characteristics really accurately.

Once you have completed the analysis, identify the performance elements you would most like to improve. Multiple goals are
most effective so try six to ten elements at first. Now decide *how
much* you want to improve each element and *by when*. Make sure
these goals challenge you but remain realistic. As a guide to help
you decide how much improvement to aim for, try to raise your
standard so that the best performance you have achieved so far
for any particular item will only be an average performance by the
end of the programme. For instance, if your average first serve
percentage for a match is 50 per cent but you have managed 65
per cent on one occasion, work to improve your average to 65 per
cent.

How long you keep to your goal-setting programme is really up
to you, but it should be long enough to allow for a reasonable
improvement, but not so long that it feels endless. In practice,
this usually means between two weeks and three months for
most elements of performance. Within the programme, of
course, you will have separate goals for each occasion you assess
performance in addition to the final goal(s) of the programme.

The most difficult part of a goal-setting programme is deciding
how the improvement can be achieved. As far as mental approach
is concerned, the answers are in this book, but consult your
coach about which training methods will bring about the desired
improvement in your skills, strategies and fitness. Once you
embark on this programme it is very important to keep full and
accurate records.

The principles of setting goals

Before we continue, this is a good time to recap on some of the
important points. To get the most out of setting goals for
yourself, remember the principles which govern their effectiveness. The acronym **SCAMP** may help you.

S   **Specific.** Don't set yourself vague goals such as 'improve-
       ment'. Specify how much you want to improve and how you
       can measure it. Predict the extent of your improvement and
       you will work hard to achieve it.

C **Challenging** and **Controllable.** Goals should remain within the realms of possibility but you need to challenge yourself. There is conclusive research that specific, challenging goals produce better performance than easy goals or no goals at all. Also, try to keep the objectives you set yourself within your personal control. Too many athletes use winning rather than personal performance as a reference point. Winning is controlled partly by someone else's performance. You have almost total control over your own performance. Even losing efforts can and should allow for goal attainment.

A **Attainable.** Don't burden yourself with an impossible goal. All goals should relate to where you are now and you should aim to improve yourself step by step. Don't be afraid to reassess your goals if they prove unrealistic.

M **Measurable** and **Multiple.** The sense of achievement is greatest, and motivation enhanced most, when progress can actually be seen. Goals should therefore be expressed in a form which can be measured by some objective test. Failing that, you can measure performance on a subjective rating scale of one to ten. Remember that multiple goals increase the probability of achievement. It's a good feeling to tick off items achieved from a list of things to do. Every training session should include smaller goals which contribute to some final objective.

P **Personal.** The goals you set must relate to you as an individual. Decide what *you* want to achieve; don't borrow other people's goals. This will enhance your commitment to those objectives.

A complete programme for setting goals

By now you should be ready to design your own **Performance enhancement programme**. You will be able to chart your improvement and you will have accepted personal responsibility for your own development in sport. All these are important steps on the road to fulfilling your potential.

Study the example in exercise 4 carefully before you complete the exercise. Note that the weaknesses which must be improved were identified from the performance analysis score sheet,

Performance enhancement programme example

Name: Colin Beecher   Age: 17

Sport: Tennis   Date: 1 September 1988

Standard: Junior international

Dates

Skills	Test	Training	SCORE	Goal	Score	Goal	Score	Goal	Score	Goal	Score	Goal	Score	Goal	Score	Goal	Score	Goal	Score	Goal	Score	Goal	Score
Serve	Point system related	15 mins per day extra practice	48	50	52	54	56	56	56	59	61	64	67	70									70
Rt groundstrokes	to target area on court	Video analysis required practice	52	56	58	58	60	62	64	64	68	69	70										
High volley	Percentage & maximum score	15 mins per day intensive practice	44	48	50	55	56	58	62	65	68	70										
Strategies																						
Approaching net	Scale 1–10	Video analysis/spec coaching	5	5.5	6	6	6	6.5	6.5	6.5	7	7	7.5	7.5	8								
Footwork	"	Skipping programme & spec coaching	5	5.5	6	6	6	6.5	6.5	6.5	7	7	7.5	7.5	8								
Fitness																						
Speed	Tennis court shuttle	2×1½ hr session/week. High intensity training	9.9	9.6	9.4	9.2	4.1	4.0	3.9	3.9	8.8	8.7	8.7	8.5									
Suppleness	Sit and reach	Stretching programme	4	6	8	9	10	11	12	13	14	15	16										
Mental approach																						
Confidence	Scale 1–10	Confidence building exercises	6	6.5	6.5	6.5	7	7	7	7.5	7.5	7.5	9										
Coolness under pressure	"	Relaxation programme	4	4.5	5	5.5	5	6	6	6.5	7	7.5	9										

Performance enhancement programme

Name: _____ Age: _____

Sport: _____ Date: _____

Standard: _____

	Test	Training
Skills		
Strategies		
Fitness		
Mental approach		

Dates

SCORE	Goal	Score	Goal	Score	Goal	Score	Goal	Score	Goal	Score	Goal	Score	Goal	Score	Goal	Score	Goal	Score	Goal	Score

Exercise 4

PEP is modified from the Achievement Management Plan in Singer, R. N. (1984) *Sustaining Motivation in Sport*. Sport Consultants International, FL.

where they were marked with an asterisk. These scores were entered on the Performance enhancement programme to act as the basis on which improvement would be measured. Weekly goals were then established and this encouraged gradual progression towards a realistic target over a ten-week period. If this final target has been set too high or low it can be re-assessed as you go along.

Personal contracts

If your motivation for a particular element of your programme is very low, try making a contract with yourself. This involves exploiting the sense of duty and obligation which most people have. If we make appointments we usually try to keep to them, and the more formal the commitment the more likely we are to honour it. For instance, if you arrange to meet someone in a particular place, at a particular time, on a particular date, you are far more likely to actually get to see that person than if you had simply agreed to 'meet sometime next week'. By formalizing the arrangement, you are making a contract with yourself and a particular time is therefore booked. Most of us will abide by such a contract, even if it subsequently proves to be a bit inconvenient.

This system works equally well in enhancing motivation for sport. By making contracts with yourself you increase the chances of fulfilling a task and the more formal the contract, the more it will appeal to your sense of duty. For example, if you are a person who finds it difficult to knuckle down to serious fitness training, try committing yourself to a written contract of the sort shown in the following examples. Alternatively, if there is another aspect of your sport you wish to increase your commitment to, use these examples as a guide and draw up a contract with yourself which will improve the situation. Ask someone close to you to witness the contract and then place it in a prominent position so that you are frequently reminded of your commitment. Make sure you enter these appointments in your diary to prevent you from double booking.

Having a regular training partner can also increase your commitment to training, but beware of the possibility that if your training partner drops out for some reason you will be tempted to do the same. Ideally, therefore, your contract should be, first and foremost, with yourself.

Personal contracts

Example 1

I, the undersigned, do hereby promise that I shall devote every Tuesday and Thursday evening, from 6.30 to 8.00 p.m. for a three-month period commencing 1st September, to fitness training at the City Sports Centre.

Signed _____

Witnessed _____

Example 2

I, _____, promise to continue early morning swimming at 7.30 a.m. daily at the Newtown swimming baths until I have managed to complete 800 metres in under 15 minutes on three consecutive days.

Signed _____

Witnessed _____

Once you have fulfilled a contract, reward yourself in some small way, perhaps by taking a day off, or treating yourself to a favourite meal. Then make another, perhaps more challenging, contract with yourself. You should not make your new obligations *too* demanding. They must always remain realistic, and above all it is vital that you fulfil your original commitments otherwise the impetus will be lost. With each contract fulfilled you will gain a sense of achievement and gradually commitment will grow to the point where you will no longer allow yourself to break a contract. You are looking for a snowball effect where the fulfillment of each task generates greater and greater motivation for the next task.

Token rewards

Token rewards are small prizes which have little or no actual worth but which symbolize achievement, and which can therefore attain great value. 'Player of the Year' awards, the 'House Colours' given in some schools, and even Olympic medals are all token rewards and carry with them tremendous prestige and honour. As a motivational strategy, token rewards are clearly suitable for use by coaches trying to motivate teams of players, but with a little imagination can be adapted by individuals to improve their own performance.

As a consultant to the Lawn Tennis Association, one of my responsibilities is to improve the speed and agility of International Junior players. Speed drills are by their very nature repetitive and to be effective they must be performed at very close to maximum effort. Motivation is an inevitable problem in these situations and token rewards offer a simple but very effective solution. After spending time on flexibility and technique work, each speed session includes shuttle races or straight sprints. In an effort to make these more rewarding I started to 'award' gold, silver and bronze medals to the first three in each drill. In reality no prize was awarded other than announcing the result to the group. The effect was immediately noticeable. This simple system ensures maximum effort because all the participants know that their efforts are being noted and rewarded. It also appeals to the fantasy figure within us who dreams of Olympic glory, and, most importantly, the 'medals' soon gain status amongst the group to the extent that a close count is kept of medal tables by the athletes themselves.

On their initiation a system grew up whereby players could 'play their joker' for double medals on a particular race (a gimmick borrowed from television's *It's a Knockout*).

It is very important that everyone has a chance to share in the glory. Remember that competition only acts as a motivator to those participants who believe that they have a chance of winning. In a small group, everyone will usually believe that they have a chance of finishing in the first three, but if an imbalance of talent is obvious then relays provide the answer. By carefully pairing or grouping the players then teams of approximately equal ability can be arranged. By manipulating the groupings and varying the event, it is usually possible to ensure that everyone wins something. At the end of each session I award 'Man of the Day' status to the player who performed best relative to his ability. I try to share this around but the system must be seen to be fair. Usually by listening to the players' comments to one another it is easy to work out who gets the popular vote. After two years of this system the prestige attached to 'Man of the Day' is remarkable.

To be successful, such a system requires consistency above all else. The trainer must be judge, referee and commentator all in one. Enthusiasm is infectious and any player who is cynical about the scheme will become enthusiastic when he wins a medal. Try to make a fuss of those who show the greatest personal improvement, regardless of whether they are the best or not. To make token rewards an effective way of increasing motivation follow the following guidelines, and try to remember **SCORE**:

S **Simplicity** Don't go overboard with the complexity of the system. A very simple reward system which is run well is more effective than one which is difficult to understand.

C **Consistency** As a leader you must be seen to be fair. Favouritism or inconsistency in applying the reward will kill its effectiveness.

O **Observation** Everyone must be assured that their efforts will be noticed. This encourages those who are really trying and discourages those who might otherwise think they needn't bother.

R **Reward** Keep the reward in perspective. Remember it need only be public recognition that a particular individual has achieved something. It needs no actual worth. We all worked hard to win gold stars at infant school and the same principle applies to older children or adults.

E **Explanation** Explain to all concerned what you are seeking to improve and then highlight the exact reward system being used. For example, 'For every fitness exercise on which you beat your score of last week you get one point. The person with most points is "Trainer of the Week".' It is crucial that everyone understands what is required to win the reward.

It should be clear to you by now that improved performance is closely related to increased effort. In fact it is part of your education in the art of winning to realize just how much performance *depends* upon effort. But do not use up effort aimlessly.

Motivation grows as it becomes clear that effort is being re-warded. If you set goals, this will demonstrate that improvement is taking place and will leave you in no doubt that your efforts are paying dividends.

Before you proceed, be sure to complete the exercises in this chapter, or at the very least, to make a contract with yourself that you will fulfil these tasks by a set time in the very near future. Taking charge of your own progress is an important step for-wards. The next, vital step towards a winning mentality is to believe, no matter how unlikely it seems at times, that your success in sport is directly controllable, by your decisions and your actions.

HOW VISUALIZATION CAN IMPROVE PERFORMANCE

Throughout history, human achievement has relied on our capacity to look beyond where we are now, to see what might be possible. Everything which is now proved was once only imagined and every discovery now taken for granted was made possible only by someone's foresight and vision. When you next look out over a flat landscape, consider how likely a round earth really seems. Would you have dared venture around the globe in ancient times or would you have played safe for fear of falling off the edge?

Sporting achievements are also dependent upon the ability to create in the mind that which has not yet been achieved, and a dull, inactive imagination always inhibits progress. However modest or mighty your sporting ambitions might be, you should already have been there many times in your imagination, because if you cannot even imagine them, how can you hope to achieve them? To fulfil your true sporting potential you will need to take control of your imagination and use it to advantage.

The true force of imagination is revealed in dreams and nightmares where images are often so vivid that you may be woken up in a cold sweat. But imagination has an equally real effect upon our conscious lives. It has the power to release hidden strengths and even to inhibit totally. Therefore the more you control imagination, the more you will control performance. Remember that if you can see it you can create it; if you can feel it you can perform it; if you can imagine it you can achieve it.

To use imagination constructively involves much more than idle daydreaming. Only when the imagination is used skilfully and systematically to help create or to revive the ultimate performance will you benefit. Imagination channelled in this disciplined way is referred to as visualization or imagery, and although at first mention it may sound a bit complicated, in reality, imagery is a simple concept with very basic applications.

WHAT IS VISUALIZATION?

Visualization involves freeing the creative side of the brain so that you think without the need for words. Although this usually means creating pictures in the mind, or 'seeing with your mind's eye', there are several different perspectives for using imagery. Described here are three common perspectives which athletes might use to create or recreate sporting experiences:

Visual-internal This form of imagery involves viewing what is going on around you as you would if you were actually there performing. A downhill skier, for instance, using this form of 'first person' visualization would view each bump and turn approaching in his or her imagined run down the mountain and would see the scenery flashing by as though his or her eyes were a camera.

Visual-external In contrast, this form of imagery is like watching yourself through a camera. It is 'third person' visualization where you step outside yourself momentarily to watch yourself perform. Here the downhill skier would picture him- or herself hurtling down the mountain crouched in the tuck position, carving turns or jumping, as though seeing themselves on *Ski Sunday*. This is the most common imagery perspective used by athletes.

Kinesthetic This form of imagery involves recreating the physical feeling of performance. The downhill skier would imagine the feeling of pushing the heels back and the shins forward in the skiboot, would feel the sensation in the knees as bumps were hit and the thigh muscles starting to burn towards the end of a long run.

You will probably have a natural inclination towards one or other of these different visualization perspectives but, because each one relies heavily on a single sensory mechanism (either sight or feel), none of them fully exploits the true potential of imagery. The best use of imagery involves a complete sensory experience which uses our senses of taste, smell and hearing, as well as those of sight and feel. For example, if you were a tennis player using imagery to recreate the experience of serving, you should imagine the feeling of stretching up and swinging the racket, the sound of the ball as you hit it, the smells in the air and the taste of sweat, in addition to seeing yourself perform the action.

To date, research is very unclear about which forms of visualization are most useful to performers, although some trends are emerging. In sports such as gymnastics or diving where performers move at their own pace in an environment which does not change, it appears that successful performers tend to employ kinesthetic imagery rather than visual imagery when mentally rehearsing skills. In other words, they seem to benefit more from recreating the *feel* of movements than from generating a mental *picture*.

On the other hand, sports such as skiing, which require the performer to respond to a quickly changing environment, and sports such as squash, badminton, soccer and hockey, where the performer reacts to an opponent, all appear to benefit more from visual imagery than from kinesthetic imagery.

However, there are certainly no hard and fast rules about using visualization, and becoming proficient in the widest range of techniques is the most sensible policy whatever your sport. Ultimately, the acid test for any form of visualization must be whether it is effective for you. The simple advice is, 'if you find that it works, use it!'

WHY DOES VISUALIZATION BENEFIT PERFORMANCE?

As a sane person you no doubt think of yourself as being able to distinguish between events which happen in reality and those which are only imagined. In fact the distinction is much less obvious than you might believe. The messages sent, in the form of neural impulses, to and from the brain during imagined action closely resemble those messages sent during physical action.

If you visualize yourself performing any skill, this causes electromyographical (EMG) activity in those muscle groups, similar to that which would occur during the physical performance of the imagined movement. For example, if you were to visualize yourself raising an arm out to the side it would be possible to monitor activity in the deltoid muscles even though no physical movement occurs.

Imagery therefore has the effect of 'priming' the appropriate muscles for subsequent physical action, and this clearly has potential benefits for the performance of many sports skills. Also, the neural impulses passed from the brain to the muscular system during visualization may be retained in memory almost as if the movement had actually occurred. This means that physical skills may be improved even when they are only practised in the mind.

The number of ways in which visualization can be used to benefit sports performance and skill development is limited only by your own powers of imagination. This chapter outlines several common applications of visualization techniques but with practice and a little ingenuity you will be able to devise many others.

INDIVIDUAL DIFFERENCES IN VISUALIZATION ABILITY

Our ability to use visualization varies greatly. Some people can evoke only visual images, others can more readily imagine how actions feel. The fortunate ones are able to recreate experiences using all five senses. People also vary in the vividness of their imagery and the degree to which they can control action during visualization. Some cannot hold a clear picture in their mind for any length of time, nor can they create moving images effectively. Similarly, while most people are able to visualize in colour, others are restricted to black and white images. Like most aspects of human functioning, the use of imagery is a skill which some individuals naturally find easier than others, but in common with all skills, anyone can develop effective imagery with sufficient practice.

As you attempt to develop your visualization skills you should aim for maximum vividness and maximum controllability. The more clearly you experience mental images and the more accurately you can control these imagined movements, the more likely you are to translate these images into improved performance. The following exercise is a preliminary one to help you explore your own methods of visualization. The exercise takes you through a whole range of senses and you will probably notice that visualization is easier for you with some senses than with others. You may need to repeat this exercise several times before you become proficient at creating and controlling vivid images in your mind, but do persevere. Remember that Rome wasn't built in a day.

Introduction to visualization

This exercise is a simple introduction to visualization skills which will help you to understand your own methods of visualizing things. It will identify which senses you can best imagine with, which ones are most vivid, and which ones you can control best.

Before you start, sit in a comfortable chair and relax by closing your eyes, breathing slowly and deeply and allowing the tension to leave your muscles as you exhale. Spend a few minutes doing this until you feel really relaxed.

Now you are going to imagine a series of sounds, feels, smells, tastes and sights. Take time to explore each image and enjoy the experience.

Sounds
- The crunch as you bite into a crisp apple
- The crash of breaking glass
- The plop of a pebble dropped into a pond
- The sound of a tennis ball on the sweet spot of a raquet.

Feels
- The dimpled skin of an orange
- The fur on a new tennis ball
- The coldness of fresh snow
- The slippery smoothness of soap.

Smells
- The aroma of freshly ground coffee
- The fragrance of your favourite perfume or after shave
- The heavy smell of chlorine as you enter an indoor swimming pool
- The smell of newly mown grass on a hot summer's day.

Tastes
- The sweetness of honey
- The bitterness of dark chocolate
- The sharpness of a lemon
- The taste of salt on the tip of your tongue.

Sights
- A majestic snowcapped mountain
- All the colours of the rainbow, one after another: red, orange, yellow, green, blue, indigo, violet
- Your favourite ride at the funfair
- You performing sit-ups.

Try to identify which senses are vivid and which ones are difficult to evoke. Can you see movement in your images? Are you able to visualize in colour? Make brief notes in answer to these questions and write down anything else which seemed important about your images. This will be useful information in subsequent imagery exercises.

Now try using all five senses to create images. Start with something simple like making and then drinking a cup of coffee. Then try to recreate the experience of performing sit-ups or press-ups. It may help to physically perform the action and then recreate it in your mind immediately afterwards. Repeat the exercise once a day until your visualization becomes vivid and easily controllable.

USING VISUALIZATION DURING TRAINING

Visualization has several applications during the long hours of training. Not only can it be used to learn new skills but it also assists in the development of existing skills, and it has an important part to play in improving tactical awareness.

Learning a new skill

When learning a new skill, visualization has two very specific uses. Firstly, when you observe a demonstration of the skill to be learned it pays to run through your own slow-motion replay of the movement, placing yourself in the role of performer. This can help to fix the basic movement pattern in your memory before you even attempt the movement physically. It is, however, vital that the demonstration you observe is a good one because mentally practising a poorly executed skill will do more harm than good.

Secondly, visualization can be used to remember important details about the skill. For instance, if you were learning to swim breast stroke, it would help to be told to think of kicking through the water like a frog. A simple image like this always conveys so much more about the technique than an elaborate explanation ever can. The same applies to the back scratch position in the tennis serve, which captures the correct movement pattern with a splendid economy of detail.

The more images replace explanation in learning the more simply and effectively techniques will be mastered and the quicker learning will progress. Whether you are in the position of teacher or learner, visualization has a big part to play in communicating and understanding skills. If you can capture the heart of a skill in a simple image, practice becomes much easier.

Developing tactical awareness

Skills where the emphasis is on thought processes rather than physical movement benefit most from mental practice. For instance, repeating a telephone number over and over to yourself is much more likely to fix it in memory than physically dialling the number several times. In chess, the whole essence of the contest is to outfox your opponent by playing the game in your head many moves in advance, and the physical movements of the pieces on the board simply confirm the outcome of the mental visualization. Therefore, the control of images determines skill level in chess rather than the physical skill of moving the pieces.

Team games such as American football, rugby, soccer and hockey, with their intricacies and strategies are a bit like giant games of chess. So, for the coach or player who is responsible for deciding tactics, visualization is an important means of exploring the potential effectiveness of various moves and counter moves.

Mental practice can also be useful for team members to rehearse their role in each set play, and to practice reacting to every eventuality until it becomes second nature. Using visualization to increase your familiarity with a wide range of tactical situations means that when they occur in reality your reactions will be faster. Less information needs to be processed before the situation is recognized for what it is, and the appropriate response can therefore be initiated more quickly.

Practising existing skills

As mentioned earlier, research has shown that when you visualize performing an action, the muscles which you would use if you were performing the action physically are activated in much the same way. This means that the movement patterns which you may be attempting to perfect can be practised in the absence of physical movement and yet still be retained in memory. As you practice mentally, your muscles are to some extent rehearsing the movement. You are literally thinking with your body as well as with your mind.

Just consider the potential advantages of developing physical skills through mental practice. Practice has long since been established as the most important factor in skill development, and mental practice can be performed anywhere, at any time. It requires no equipment, and can take place even when you are injured. This does not mean, of course, that mental practice is as beneficial as physical practice, but it is certainly better than no practice at all, and a combination of mental and physical practice is better than physical practice alone.

It would be wrong to think of mental practice as being an easier option than physical practice. Remember that visualizing is not the same as daydreaming. Visualization is a skill in itself which needs considerable practice before it becomes effective. But with planning and effort, mental practice has been shown to contribute significantly to skill development, and because it causes no fatigue it is sometimes possible to progress more rapidly than one would with physical practice.

Individual sports, such as figure skating, archery, shooting and gymnastics, lend themselves particularly to mental practice. This is because they involve no direct interaction with opponents, and so the actual competition environment can be reproduced in the mind with a high degree of accuracy. However, many other less predictable sports have also been shown to benefit from mental practice. Basketball players, for instance, have demonstrated significant improvements to their free throw success rate after supplementing physical practice with mental practice, while swimmers and track athletes perfect their pacing of races by running through them in their minds several times.

James Mays, who so often acts as pacemaker to the stars of track athletics in their world record attempts, spends a lot of time practising his races mentally to ensure that the pace he sets is right on schedule. He talks about it as 'a mind game, where I shut my eyes, start my watch, then imagine running the first lap and stopping the watch at 400 metres. Usually I'm no more than a second out.'

The next exercise outlines basic guidelines for practising sports skills mentally, but before you start, spend time deciding upon the particular skill you wish to improve and plan the mental practice session very thoroughly. Include the imaginary conditions in which you will practise, the exact number of times you will repeat the skill, and the goals you are trying to achieve in the session. When practising mentally remember to call upon all your senses to make the image as real as possible.

Practising skills mentally

Planning the session

- Decide on a specific skill you wish to improve

- Identify the practice environment as precisely as you can. It is better if the imagined practice were to take place somewhere which is familiar enough for you to recall the sights, sounds and smells. Is it indoors or outdoors? If it is outdoors, what are the weather conditions? What time of day is it?

- Clarify the content of the practice. How many times are you going to practice this skill? Will you be opposed or unopposed? With others or alone?

- Set yourself a performance goal. This should relate to your present level of skill. Don't set out to produce perfection during mental practice but do make sure you achieve your performance goal. The practice should always be realistic but successful

- Schedule the mental practice session. Mental practice can take place anywhere, at any time, but it is best if it does not clash with some other activity. Make use of otherwise wasted time such as a long journey or a lunch break. Setting aside a regular time is the best policy

Mental practice record
(example)

Plan

Skill being practised: Rugby goal-kicking, RH, 30 yds out .
Practice environment: Home ground, kicking towards club-
house

Conditions: Dry, windy (L→R)   Time of day: 3·00 pm

No. of repetitions: 50   Opposed (O) or Unopposed (U):

Performance goal: 30/50 successful
(e.g. Number of successful attempts, rating out of 10 for
style.)

Date and time of session: Monday, 6·00 pm

Notes (*fill in after session*):

Level of performance: 36/50 Started off poorly but finished
well

Important details of technique: Kept approach run straight,
5-stride approach. Leaned away, used L arm to balance.
Non-kicking foot just behind ball. Aimed just inside RH post
Arc cancelled by breeze
Kinesthetic feelings: Could feel a long swing of kicking leg
on successful attempts. Aware of exact point of impact on foot.
Could tell whether kick was going to be good or bad.

Emotions: Started off feeling nervous so fluffed one or two
early attempts. Relaxed later and got into a good rhythm
Felt very confident towards the end.

Mental practice record

Plan

Skill being practised: _____
Practice environment: _____

Conditions: _____   Time of day: _____

No. of repetitions: _____   Opposed (O) or Unopposed (U):

Performance goal: _____
(e.g. Number of successful attempts, rating out of 10 for style.)

Date and time of session: _____

Notes (*fill in after session*):

Level of performance: _____

Important details of technique: _____
_____
_____

Kinesthetic feelings: _____
_____
_____

Emotions: _____
_____
_____

Exercise 5

- Enter the plan of your session on the 'Mental practice record' in exercise 5, using the example as a guide.

Practising skills mentally

Starting the session

- Before you start, spend a few minutes relaxing. Lie down or sit down comfortably and focus on your breathing. Close your eyes and breathe deeply, inhaling to a count of four, holding your breath for a count of four, and exhaling to a count of eight. Let go of any tension as you count. Say 'relax' to yourself as you breathe in and 'let go' as you breathe out

- Once you are relaxed, begin by creating a picture in your mind's eye of the practice environment. Recreate exactly what you can see when you are there, the sounds you can hear, and any tastes, smells or feelings you associate with the scene

- Visualize yourself coming into view. Notice what you are wearing. Listen to the sound of your footsteps. Begin your usual warm-up routine. Perhaps a short jog followed by some stretching exercises . . . notice your heartrate increasing and your muscles starting to loosen

- Now picture yourself commencing practice. Prepare for each attempt in the same way and at the same pace as you would if you were performing the skill in reality. As you repeat the movement over and over again, pay close attention to how it feels to perform this skill . . . what are the feelings in your arms . . . in your legs . . . throughout your body? See and feel yourself performing better than you have ever managed before

- Once you have completed the designated number of attempts (you should aim for a minimum of about 50) jot down a few notes about the mental practice session. Did you achieve your performance goal? What things stick in your mind about performing the skill so successfully . . . what aspects of technique were you aware of . . . what internal feelings . . . what emotions?

- Try to follow up the mental practice session with physical practice of the same skill as soon as possible. This combination of mental practice followed by physical practice has been shown to be the most effective method of developing skills.

PREPARING FOR COMPETITION

In any sporting contest, particularly those between evenly matched opponents, it is impossible to predict the outcome with absolute certainty. Competitive sport is always, to some extent, a venture into the unknown. This is especially true if the contest takes place at an unfamiliar venue, or in unexpected conditions, or against an opponent of unknown qualities. An appearance at Wembley stadium, for instance, in front of a huge, impassioned crowd is, for most players, unlike anything they have ever experienced before. Wembley cup finals and international debuts are notorious for causing players to either freeze with fear or to rush around like the proverbial headless chicken.

Very few players perform to the best of their ability on their first appearance in such circumstances. Because they don't know exactly what to expect, players will experience a certain type of fear, and that throws the body's defence systems into confusion. The human body reacts to threatening situations by releasing hormones, such as adrenalin, that helps you to either face up to a situation or to run away from it. This is often referred to as the preparation for 'fight or flight'. It is irrelevant whether the threat is real or only imagined.

The unknown is perceived as being threatening. Therefore, the more elements of the unknown which are present in a sporting situation, the more likely the adrenalin is to flow. In general, this helps performance because the release of the hormone increases blood supply to the muscles and reduces sensations of pain, but it is very easy to become over-excited or anxious, either of which can lead to poorer performance. Because of the inherent unpredictability of sport, any sporting occasion, from a kick around on the green to the World Cup Final can potentially be seen as threatening. Sometimes it is a threat to the body which is perceived, but more often it is a threat to the ego.

Visualization can be used to reduce the unknown from an upcoming contest, thereby deflecting this sense of threat. You can achieve this by creating in your mind the complete competition experience from the moment you enter the changing room before the contest to the time you return there after victory. It is important to use all your senses to make the experience as real as possible, and to run through the visualization at normal speed if this is feasible. If the contest would normally last for five minutes then the visualization should last for five minutes.

Avoid indulging yourself in unrealistic fantasy. Make sure to keep your imagery in line with what you can realistically expect, based on what you already know about your opponent, the situation and yourself. Include in your visualization the inevitable mistakes which you are bound to make and decide how you will cope with them in advance. Experience moments when the contest appears to be slipping away from you and analyse how to regain control. You need to anticipate every eventuality and decide in advance the best way to handle it. Not only does this remove any fear of the unknown, but it prepares you to respond in the most effective manner to the ups and downs of competition.

VISUALIZING BEFORE THE PERFORMANCE

Visualizing yourself performing a skill just prior to performing it physically is known as *mental rehearsal*. It is a very simple and effective application of visualization. Running through a successful attempt in your mind immediately before performing will remove doubt at the crucial moment and will also fine tune the body for action by priming the required muscle groups.

In common with most high jumpers, British record holder Geoff Parsons is a proponent of mental rehearsal. Before each attempt he will run through the complete jump in his mind several times, seeing in great detail each deliberate stride of his run-up, the upward surge of his leading leg and arms at take-off, and, most importantly, a successful clearance. Only when the bar has been beaten mentally will the jump be attempted physically.

Another celebrated visualizer is golfer Jack Nicklaus, who claims that he never hits a golf shot without running it in his mind

Geoff Parsons

first. To use his phrase, he 'goes to the movies in his head', allowing each stroke to flow through his mind in reverse. First he clarifies exactly where he wants the ball to land and then he imagines its flight path to that precise spot. Only then will he visualize the particular swing required to produce the shot. This use of visualization has become an integral part of his preparation for every golf shot he plays.

> I never hit a shot, even in practice, without having a very sharp, in-focus picture of it in my head. It's like a colour movie. First I 'see' the ball where I want it to finish, then the scene quickly changes and I 'see' the ball going there, then there's a sort of fade-out, and the next scene shows me making the kind of swing that will turn the previous images into reality.

The order of events he describes is important because the last thing he visualizes just prior to playing a shot is the swing itself. This keeps the movement pattern fresh in his memory. Other golfers attempt to capture the essence of the required swing by visualizing an arc of light as the line that the club head will follow. When actually playing the shot, the player can concentrate solely on taking the club head back along this illuminated line. This visualization technique can be adapted quite easily to suit a wide variety of skills.

When using mental rehearsal, try to develop the conviction that if you can visualize it happening then it will happen in reality. Naturally mental rehearsal does not guarantee a successful outcome, but it does increase the chance of you producing your best effort. If something disturbs your rehearsal or the visualized attempt is unsuccessful, start the process again until you visualize a successful performance of the skill.

VISUALIZING DURING PERFORMANCE

Although mental rehearsal is usually considered in the context of self-paced skills, where the performer has time to prepare before each movement, many famous players in very spontaneous sports report using imagery even *during* fast-moving action. Billie-Jean King, for example, said:

I see one coming and visualize just where I'm going to hit it
and the shot's perfect – and I feel beautiful all over.

However, it is probably during endurance events that imagery
can do most to sustain a high level of performance from the body
when the mind starts to feel like giving up. During most endurance events there comes a point where the battle between the
body and the mind begins to rage. When the body starts to
complain, the mind can either cope with the discomfort or
succumb to the body's demands to ease up. There are two ways
in which visualization can play a part in the coping process.
Firstly, it can help you dissociate yourself from the situation
causing the discomfort. For instance, controlled experiments
have shown that athletes performing endurance tasks while
visualizing themselves lying on a beach or strolling along a
riverbank, actually believe they are working less hard than when
they perform the same task while focusing on their bodily signals
of discomfort.

This dissociation strategy is very common amongst 'ultra-
marathoners', a rare breed of dedicated athletes who run distances of 50, 100 or even 200 miles non-stop. Such extraordinary
feats of endurance become a test of mental ruggedness more
than of physical conditioning and visualization is an important
factor in performance. Many ultra-marathoners engage in very
complex mental arithmetic to keep their attention directed away
from the pain. Some create poetry in their minds, others may
make detailed plans for an extension to their house. All of these
involve a disciplined use of imagery to help them ignore the
body's constant messages of discomfort.

Visualization can also be used to help you sustain effort all the
way to the finishing line in less protracted but equally discomfort-
ing events. Visualizing a huge hand helping you along can make
the effort seem just that little bit easier, or picturing yourself
being 'reeled in' towards the finishing line by some giant's fishing
rod can also help cope with the strain.

Many athletes report using heroic imagery to sustain effort in
the face of adversity. Images of Olympic glory, or of getting
despatches through to HQ, or any personal image which conveys
to you the notion that 'when the going gets tough, the tough get
going', will help to dredge your reserves of will-power and
determination. Remember that the body will only cease trying
when the mind tells it to, and there is an endless list of people who

have overcome seemingly impossible odds through sheer dog-
gedness. Even Napoleon acknowledged that 'the spirit in the long
run will always conquer the sword', and the trick, therefore, is to
identify those personal images which rouse your spirit in moments of difficulty.

VISUALIZING AFTER PERFORMANCE

Smart athletes realize that every performance, good or bad, is an
opportunity to learn. Even the most disappointing defeat can be
transformed into a valuable experience if something positive can
be extracted from it. Using visualization to recreate a replay of
your performance often proves to be the simplest and most
effective method of analysing it.

At a conscious level it is sometimes very difficult to recall
precise details of a performance. The more you master the skills
of a sport the less conscious thought you require to produce
those skills, and the more of your attention you devote to tactical
considerations. In effect, high level performers produce skills
almost automatically, and because this gives them more time to
gather information about situations, they are able to make
correct decisions earlier and to anticipate the movements of
opponents better. However, this mastery of skills can on occasions be a double-edged sword.

Producing skills unconsciously means reduced awareness of
the mechanisms by which skills are generated and this can lead to
difficulties in identifying faults in technique. Basically, because
the highly skilled devote less thought to how the skills are
produced, they are less aware of the small changes in technique
which creep in over time. This can leave even champion athletes
confused and despondent after a poor performance. Admittedly,
this is a relatively small price to pay for the advantages which
these skills will give you as a performer, but nonetheless you will
find it very frustrating when a technical fault arises and you are
unable to identify its exact cause. The trained eye of a very
experienced coach is usually required to identify faults among
these top performers, but this may prove difficult or costly to
arrange. Video analysis is another way of reviewing the finer

points of performance but again this may prove to be an unrealistic proposition.

Visualization often proves the most effective compromise. Conducting your own detailed replays of poor performance often provides the clue to technical faults which you would otherwise remain unaware of. Using imagery in this way will also help to identify which patterns of behaviour or methods of preparation contribute to good and bad performances. The mental practice procedure described earlier can easily be modified for performance analysis.

Performance analysis exercise

Plan and start the session in the same way as you would for mental practice, but while you are visualizing yourself performing, slow the movement down and go through a mental checklist of all the important technical aspects of the skill in question. For example, Fatima Whitbread might visualize herself running up, withdrawing the javelin, lengthening her stride, getting her legs ahead of her body, then driving and twisting the hips as her arm comes through long and fast. In slow motion her visualization

Fatima Whitbread

might reveal that her 'snap' with the hips was too laboured to unleash the javelin with full power, and therefore that is where she should concentrate her efforts on the next attempt.

When analysing performance during imagery, it is a good idea to capture the key elements of technique with 'labels' which act as vivid reference points during subsequent performance. For example, just prior to take-off, long jumpers prepare to transfer forward momentum into upward momentum by lowering their centre of gravity and then generating an upward surge of the leading leg. They often capture the essence of this two-part manoeuvre with the labels 'sink' and 'drive', which neatly sums up the required process.

Increasing your awareness of critical aspects of technique in this way improves the chances of accurately identifying performance errors. Moreover, these action replays will prove just as useful for isolating reasons for outstanding performance as they are for analysing poor performance.

This chapter has outlined numerous ways in which you can use the power of your imagination to develop skills and improve performance. Naturally there are many, many other ways to profit from visualization and several of these are dealt with in later chapters. Chapter 4 shows you how to use your visualization skills to change attitudes and improve confidence, chapter 5 includes a section on how to use imagery to control anxiety, and chapter 7 explains the part imagery plays in psyching yourself up for competition.

I have tried to make clear the vast, but usually unexplored, powers of human imagination. It can be viewed as our ultimate energy, the final frontier of performance, and to leave such a resource unexploited is to limit yourself to a level of achievement which does not even resemble your full potential. Although nothing in this book will transform your performance overnight, investing time in developing psychological skills such as visualization will enable you to add a new dimension to your training programme and that will certainly pay dividends in the long run.

UNDERSTANDING
SELF-CONFIDENCE

Just as St Christopher is the patron saint of travellers, confidence is the guardian angel of performance. When self-confidence is high the path between sporting potential and sports performance is relatively smooth. As confidence wanes, so pitfalls and problems are magnified and poorer performance is the inevitable result. Almost every athlete I deal with comments on this relationship and it is clear to me that not only can loss of confidence be as damaging to sporting performance as a broken leg, but it can sometimes take even longer to recover from. Certainly, learning to maintain self-confidence is an important challenge on the road to a winning mentality.

'I'm the greatest' – Muhammad Ali

Explaining the concept of self-confidence is barely necessary. Self-confidence is so visible in some people you can almost touch it. It is apparent in the way they look, the things they say, the way they move, and the thoughts they think. The athlete of recent decades who most clearly personified confidence was probably Muhammad Ali. As Cassius Clay, the brash young Olympic champion of 1960, he coined the phrase 'I'm the greatest' and thereafter carried an aura of greatness with him, repeating the affirmation so frequently and with such conviction that even his opponents believed him. If your confidence already soars like this, it may be better to avoid reading this chapter. We'll work on the principle that 'if it ain't broke, don't fix it', so off you go, all you confident Charlies, and gather round all those who, from time to time, suffer from self-doubt.

SELF-CONFIDENCE AND YOU

Confidence can be defined as the sureness of feeling equal to the task, a sureness usually characterized by absolute belief in ability. Golfer Johnny Miller referred to this as the serenity of 'knowing that your worst shot is still going to be pretty good'. You probably know someone whose self-belief has this unshakeable quality, whose ego resists even the severest misfortunes. In such people confidence is as resilient as a squash ball: the harder the blow, the quicker they bounce back. One secret of this quality is a realistic attitude towards performance. Acknowledging that bad performances are inevitable from time to time maintains the proper perspective when they do occur, strengthening rather than weakening the resolve to persist.

From the outset, it is wise to acknowledge that confidence is generally considered to be a part of personality. For rather complex reasons some individuals have more resilient self-esteem than others. Some tend to think the worst of themselves, others are more generous in their self-perceptions. Some are prone to anxiety, others are more carefree. Although these tendencies can change given time, they will not change overnight and therefore some people will always be more confident than others by nature. However, there are great fluctuations in

High
self-confidence

Low
self-confidence

confidence that are not related to personality, but are dictated by circumstances. It is these fluctuations which you can learn to control.

The first thing you should appreciate is that confidence is

specific. No one is full of confidence or totally devoid of confidence in *all* situations, or *all the time* in any particular situation. People generally have more confidence in familiar surroundings, those in which they feel at home. Even people who are normally the very epitome of confidence can lose it in a totally unfamiliar environment. Imagine Terry Wogan on a skateboard or Jack Nicklaus on a balance beam. It's a fair bet that then their self-assurance would desert them. Clearly when you take a fish out of water you expect it to flap a bit.

In the same way, a successful athlete who suffers a run of bad results for the first time, or a prolonged period of poor form, or perhaps recurrent injury problems, may perhaps experience a disturbing reaction. A new reality emerges which must be faced up to and coped with. Any football manager will tell you that 'it's a funny old game', and in all sports the pendulum of success will swing towards you one moment and away from you the next. Too often it carries your confidence with it.

THE SOURCES OF SELF-CONFIDENCE

The confidence someone feels during a particular activity or in a particular situation is generally derived from one or more of the following four sources:

- Previously successful experiences
- Being involved with the success of others
- Verbal persuasion
- The control of negative emotions.

Previously successful experiences

This really is the most important of the four. When you perform any skill successfully, you will generate confidence and will be willing to attempt something slightly more difficult. Good teachers use this principle by breaking down difficult skills into a series of tasks which progress gradually and which allow pupils to master each step before progressing on to the next. In sports such as diving and gymnastics, where performance relies very heavily on confidence, the progression to a more difficult skill is always dependent upon the previous move having been mastered successfully. Personal success breeds confidence, repeated personal failure diminishes confidence. You will utilize this principle in building your own confidence. Learning, or sometimes *re*-learning, what it feels like to be successful is a compulsory confidence-building lesson for all athletes who find themselves down in the dumps.

Being involved with the success of others

Watching other people perform successfully can also bolster your own confidence, especially if you believe that the performer closely matches your own qualities or abilities. In effect, it evokes the reaction: 'if he (or she) can do it, I can do it too'. This principle is used by all those who lead by example. Team captains are often appointed on the assumption that their confidence will rub off and will inspire those around them.

Verbal persuasion

Verbal persuasion is a fundamental means of attempting to change the attitudes and behaviour of those around us, and this includes changing their self-confidence. In sport, coaches often try to boost confidence by convincing athletes that the challenge ahead is well within their capabilities. The individual might reinforce this by repeating the message over and over to him- or herself as a form of self-persuasion. But although verbal persuasion can prove beneficial it is not nearly so potent an influence on self-confidence as the actual successful completion of a task.

The control of negative emotions

The final influence on self-confidence is the emotional response of the body to whatever situation it finds itself in. If, for instance, you become anxious about a particular contest, then your confidence will almost certainly be diminished. Sometimes this happens when an athlete returns from injury. Sometimes the importance of the occasion creates self-doubt. Maintaining confidence, therefore, is partly to do with controlling your thoughts and your emotions. Learning relaxation and concentration skills can be particularly helpful for this. (See chapters 5 and 6.)

WHAT HAPPENS WHEN CONFIDENCE DECLINES

When they lose confidence, athletes feel that their control over situations is being taken away from them. They have switched from being the puppeteer to being a puppet, and somehow someone else seems to be pulling the strings. Many athletes comment on how confidence and time are related. Those who are very confident feel as though they have an unlimited amount of time available to perform their skills, as though they are operating in a dreamy, slow-motion world, with time to observe, time to think, time to decide and time to act. As confidence seeps away, time starts to rush by. All actions feel hurried and ill-prepared, attention wavers and fluidity disappears.

Loss of confidence also allows fear to creep in. This fear may be no more than the brief thoughts of physical injury which flash through the minds of high divers, or the rugby full back's fleeting image of another broken nose as he prepares to dive on the ball at the feet of opposition players. In some sports the merest hint of fear might be enough to end careers. Grand Prix driver Nikki Lauda once said that 'emotions are what get you killed in motor racing', and James Hunt always admitted that his first priority was to 'finish racing above rather than beneath the ground'. When the stakes are this high, confidence in ability is paramount at all times.

For those returning to sport after even minor injuries, lost confidence can significantly affect performance. Going on to the rugby field with even a slight muscle strain sometimes made me feel like a knight doing battle with a piece of armour missing. More often than not, a second-rate performance or a further injury was the result.

Confidence in your physical condition will be a great influence on your performance. Resist the temptation to return to competition too soon after injury. The body has its own ways of catching you out if you do. Rehabilitating confidence after injury requires delicate handling. Later in this chapter, there is an exercise which is designed specifically for this problem.

Perhaps even more damaging to performance than the fear of physical injury is the fear of evaluation which accompanies loss of confidence. Athletes can become inhibited because of the apprehension that others will view their performance unfavourably.

Your team mates and coach are especially important here and if they are sensitive and caring people they will be supportive while you are going through a bad patch. The influence of family and friends, opponents, and sometimes spectators and the media, can quite easily make the problem worse. There has been many a professional footballer whose confidence was shattered and whose performance was ruined by taunting spectators and cruel press reports.

Remember that fear itself is the greatest villain. An over-active imagination will cause poor self-confidence. Have you noticed that when confidence is low opponents always appear bigger or faster or stronger than they really are? Imagination should be used as a powerful ally. Muhammad Ali pointed out that 'the man who have no imagination stands on the earth. He have no wings. He cannot fly.' But imagination needs to be kept on a tight rein, especially where it applies to interpreting personal events.

Whatever situation you find yourself in, remember that any occurrence is a neutral incident lacking in form or significance until we attach meaning to it. The interpretation of all events, sporting or otherwise, is a personal process. Stand in a crowd of spectators at any sporting event and it is obvious that different people attach entirely different meanings to the same occurrence.

How you interpret each element of your participation in sport is up to you, but you should realize that your imagination will have the greatest effect on your emotions and your confidence. What your senses tell you triggers off your imagination and that causes you to feel certain things, including confidence or lack of confidence. Turn this to your own advantage. Always use your imagination to search out the strengths in yourself and the weaknesses in your opponent.

Diagnosing the problem is the first step to any cure, and therefore to help you, some of the symptoms of poor self-confidence are summarized here:

- The feeling that defeat by a superior opponent is inevitable
- The feeling that control has slipped from your grasp
- The feeling that time is against you when you are performing
- The fear of physical injury
- The fear of disappointing other people

- The failure to produce your best in crucial situations
- A reduced persistence and lower intensity of effort
- The acceptance of limitations which may or may not exist in reality.

CONFIDENCE AND PERFORMANCE

It is pretty obvious to the vast majority of athletes that self-confidence enhances performance, and there is sufficient research evidence to silence the odd doubting Thomas who may question its importance. Even under strict research conditions, it has been demonstrated many times that when confidence is manipulated either up or down, there is a significant effect on sports performance.

Firstly, confident athletes are more highly motivated in terms of the persistence and intensity with which they respond to a challenge. For instance, athletes involved in experiments who were persuaded that their competitors were weaker than they actually were, beat objectively superior opponents during arm wrestling contests and other strength tests.

Similarly, confidence causes psychological barriers to evaporate. It has been shown that weightlifters perform better when they believe that the bar holds less than it actually does. This phenomenon has been exploited by coaches who have helped weightlifters lift heavier weights by convincing them that the bar held amounts they had already been able to lift.

The evidence further suggests that confidence and performance combine in a spiral relationship as illustrated in fig. 4.1. On the upward spiral, confidence is not a problem. Attitudes are positive, fear is absent, and there is a feeling of control. The result is good performance, and this further enhances confidence.

Riding the crest of any wave is an exhilarating feeling and is tinged only by the knowledge that all good things must eventually come to an end. The surfer's immediate thought when he completes a successful ride is 'How quickly can I find another wave to ride?' and in the same way, all successful athletes are

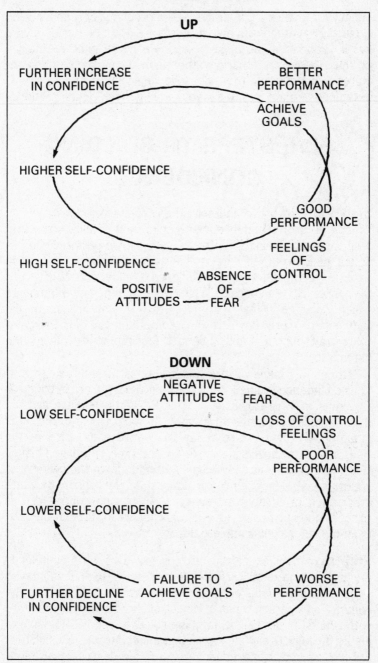

Fig 4.1

hungry for further competition. When problems of confidence do occur they invariably involve trying to break out of the downward spiral. Too often the negative attitude which poor confidence produces leads to lethargy rather than the positive action required to improve matters. The following section outlines simple but effective exercises to set you moving in the right direction.

FIVE STEPS TO BUILDING CONFIDENCE

Step one is to try to understand the precise circumstances in which you lack confidence. Self-exploration is always the first step towards regaining control over your own performance. Sit down, make yourself comfortable and review a recent sports experience which left your confidence at a low ebb. What were the exact circumstances? What were the negative thoughts which occurred? What sparked them off? How frequently did they occur? Were they related to something you did? Or something your opponent did? Spend a few moments reliving the experience.

If for some reason you are unable to recall in detail exactly how your confidence drained, then the next time you are in competition tune in very carefully to your thoughts, feelings and behaviour and make notes afterwards. If you *are* able to recall the situation vividly you are ready to complete exercise 6, the Self-confidence analysis record. By the time you have finished this you will have already begun to break down the barriers to renewed confidence. Once you understand the process by which confidence dries up you can gradually regain control of this process and start to reverse it. Carefully read through the next example before you complete this exercise.

Step two involves getting a clear grasp of what confidence means to you personally. In the next exercise (exercise 7), try to identify your personal images of confidence by writing down the name of any person, animal, object or word that you associate with confidence. It can be anything you like, you will not have to justify the logic to anyone else. Then select one image which best fits the concept of confidence for you and describe it in more detail. What qualities does he, she or it have which conveys

Self-confidence analysis record
(example)

Name: __Ian__   Sport: __Rugby__

1. Describe a sporting situation which caused your confidence to decline. A big second row forward came straight at me through the lineout. I usually put them down easily but this guy went straight through me and I was left in the mud. It happened again later in the match.

2. Write down any details about the situation which seemed especially important. He was the biggest player on the field and came at me very fast. I was slow to attack and wasn't aggressive enough. He just brushed me aside.

3. What did you imagine the significance to be?
    He was like some kind of a monster. I seemed rooted to the spot. I must have looked like a frightened poodle. My team mates must have been disgusted with me.

4. How did that make you feel?
    Small and weak and excluded from the team, as though no one wanted to pass to me.

5. Note down any other negative thoughts which passed through your mind. Express them any way you like. Use a single word or a detailed description, or even a picture if you prefer.

    Shoulder injury! A hole in the ground

Self-confidence analysis record

Name: _____   Sport: _____

1. Describe a sporting situation which caused your confidence to decline.

2. Write down any details about the situation which seemed especially important.

3. What did you imagine the significance to be?

4. How did that make you feel?

5. Note down any other negative thoughts which passed through your mind. Express them any way you like. Use a single word or a detailed description, or even a picture if you prefer.

Personal images of confidence (example)

Confidence

Gareth Edwards	Bull terrier	Mountain
Oak tree	Daley Thompson	Steam train
Carl Lewis	Piercing eyes	Grinning face
Tiger		

Best image:

Bull terrier

| Decisive | Fearless | Solid/muscular |
| Small but brave | Cool | Fast |

confidence to you? The example above will act as a guide. Spend enough time on this to build a complete image. Single descriptive words are usually as effective as elaborate explanations.

Step three involves reliving your sporting moments of supreme confidence. Replay in your mind the last time you felt really confident and successful and describe this 'winning feeling' to

Personal images of confidence

Confidence

Best image:

Exercise 7

yourself in great detail. To help you recreate the scene vividly,
refer to the visualization procedure described on pages 59 and
66. Adapt the following instructions to suit your own requirements. You may need to ask a close friend or your coach to read
them to you while you sit comfortably with your eyes closed.
Alternatively, you can make your own tape of this exercise.
Always speak slowly, clearly and in a soft voice.

1   Relax and try to re-experience the feeling of complete
    confidence.

2   Picture yourself preparing to perform.

3   Notice the sights, sounds and atmosphere of the scene. What are you wearing? What colours can you see? Are there any special noises or smells?

4   Look at your opponent(s). How does he or she appear? How does your opponent make you feel?

5   You are playing very well indeed. Pick out what is especially good about your performance.

6   Notice the score, notice the way you are moving, notice the way you feel.

7   You are playing as well as you possibly can and are feeling very confident. No one can beat you when you feel like this.

8   Notice how well you are concentrating and how relaxed your body feels.

9   Who or what do you remind yourself of when you play like this?

10 Imagine yourself playing like this for a few more moments. Everything is easy.

11 In a moment you will let the scene fade but before you do, pick out any other details which seem important.

12 Now slowly return to full awareness.

The best way to record details is to describe both the circumstances and your feelings, speaking out loud into a cassette recorder. Concentrate on describing *what* is happening and *how* you feel. When you replay your description pick out the key phrases and images which best sum up this feeling. Use them to complete exercise 8, where you summarize the winning feeling. The following example will act as a guide.

Step four is where you pinpoint the exact causes of your poor confidence and try to turn your negative thoughts into positive challenges. Notice that you will be using the Routeplanner format from page 42. This enables you to regain confidence step by step by employing the goal-setting skills you learnt earlier.

Step five is where you increase your personal control over proceedings. By now you should understand more clearly what is causing you to lose confidence, you should have clarified what

---

Your personal winning feeling
(example)

Name: Date:

Use any vivid images you can recall from visualizing your most confident performance to summarize your personal winning feeling.

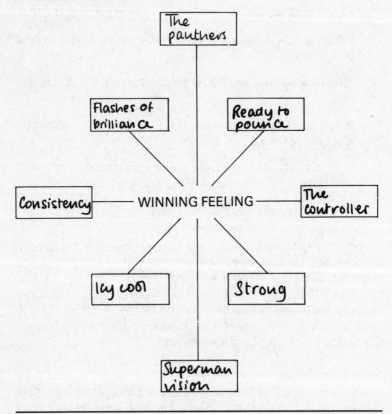

confidence means to you, and you should be more aware of what it feels like to be a winner. Exercise 9 will help you identify the obstacles which you need to overcome.

Your personal winning feeling

Name: Date:

Use any vivid images you can recall from visualizing your most confident performance to summarize your personal winning feeling.

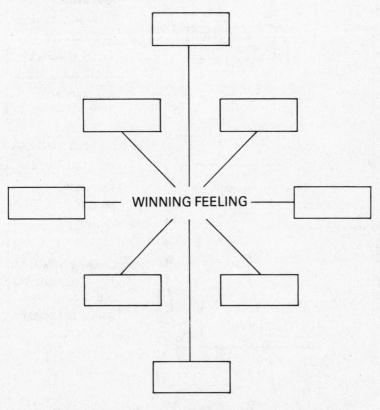

Exercise 8

Planning the route to renewed confidence

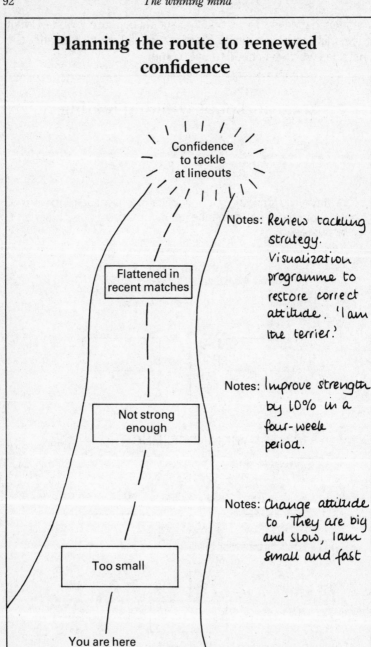

Confidence to tackle at lineouts

Flattened in recent matches

Notes: Review tackling strategy. Visualization programme to restore correct attitude. 'I am the terrier.'

Not strong enough

Notes: Improve strength by 10% in a four-week period.

Too small

Notes: Change attitude to 'They are big and slow, I am small and fast

You are here

Planning the route to renewed confidence

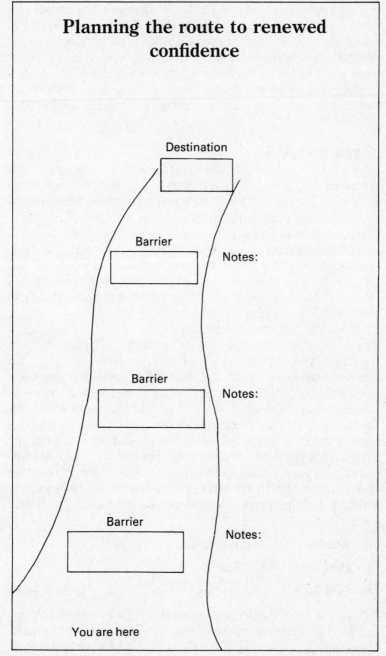

Destination

Barrier

Notes:

Barrier

Notes:

Barrier

Notes:

You are here

Exercise 9

Before you proceed, read through case study 1. This will give you some further ideas to help you complete the next exercise. Here you will identify the precise attitude you wish to achieve and the specific obstacles you will need to overcome. It is quite likely that you will not identify exactly three obstacles. This is not a problem. If there are fewer, so much the better. If there are more, just clarify them on your Routeplanner and tackle them one by one.

Case study 1

A very talented rugby scrum half, whom I have called Ian, revealed during consultation that he had recently become reluctant to tackle big opposition forwards who grabbed the ball and burst through the lineout straight at him. On several occasions his hesitation had resulted in him being flattened while trying to bring his opponent down. Both his pride and his body had been hurt each time this happened. The demoralization Ian felt had started to spread to the rest of his game and his form had slumped. Ian imagined that his team mates were also beginning to lose confidence in him.

From the self-confidence analysis record, it emerged that in these situations Ian felt that the contrast between his own physical build, which, typical of a scrum half, was small but powerful and quick, and that of taller and stronger opponents was exposed most clearly. He had begun to feel that his size and strength were not equal to the task. About 18 months before this he had sustained quite a serious shoulder injury in just this kind of situation and although the injury had cleared up long since the self-doubts persisted. The attitude Ian had once had towards tackling in these situations had gradually slipped away. Together we decided that three barriers stood between Ian's current attitude and the renewed confidence he was aiming for. These were:

● How he viewed his strength

● How he viewed his size

● How he interpreted recent attempts to tackle at the lineout.

Strength Ian's confidence in tackling big forwards was being affected adversely by the belief that his strength was inadequate. Logically, if he could improve his strength he would feel better equipped for the challenge and therefore more confident.

Consequently we devised a specific weight programme aimed at a 10 per cent overall strength gain in a four-week period.

Size Ian's concern about his physical size meant that motivating him required different tactics. As he clearly could not make himself as big as the opponents he faced, he needed to change his interpretation of the situation. We agreed that instead of thinking 'They are big, I am small', it would be better for him to foster the attitude that 'They are big and slow, I am smaller and faster'. To achieve this he visualized a variety of situations where his superior speed gave him an advantage over players who were bigger and slower.

Recent attempts to tackle Ian visualized the incident where he had sustained the shoulder injury and also the recent occasions when he had been steamrollered by opponents. In every case hesitation had seemed to contribute to the poor outcome. However, when he visualized the same situations but changed the 'script' so that he tackled without hesitation, then the outcome was successful each time. He had identified that the hesitation had created additional time which was allowing his opponents to gather momentum. This was the key factor which had made tackling more difficult.

To restore Ian's aggressive attitude towards tackling, we returned to his personal images of confidence. He had used a terrier as an image which conveyed confidence. Further prompting had revealed that a Staffordshire bull terrier was a particularly evocative image for Ian, conveying the power and aggression he wanted to restore to his game. I suggested that for a four-week period he should place a picture of a bull terrier on his bedroom wall and for 15 minutes each day he should visualize himself being that terrier. When faced with conflict, the terrier always attacked without hesitation. It was afraid of no other dog, big or small. Ian recreated what it felt like to have that attitude, and thereafter 'I am the terrier' became an effective self-statement which he used to instil aggression in himself.

By the end of the four-week period he had made significant strength gains, he was reassured that his speed gave him an advantage over lumbering forwards, and he was showing a more determined attitude towards tackling. In short, his confidence had been restored.

Now you must select the appropriate strategy for clearing each obstacle. Examples of the sorts of problems you may be faced with and the sorts of solutions which will help overcome them follow. You may need to implement several of the techniques to help along the road to full confidence. If you are willing to persevere you *will* get there in the end.

CONFIDENCE IN YOUR PREPARATION

Winning has been called the science of total preparation, and confidence certainly grows from the feeling that you are fully prepared for the task ahead. Conversely, if you have doubts about the thoroughness of your preparation for a particular contest your confidence will suffer. Total preparation refers not just to fitness, diet, and skill development but also to what might be called the logistics of competition. Timing is a crucial aspect of logistical preparation: time to travel, time to eat and time to prepare physically and mentally for the contest. Your confidence can be left in tatters if a mess is made of the arrangements and you are left short of preparation time. Forward planning and thoroughness will add an edge to your confidence.

There is also the question of clothing and equipment. The famous tennis couturier, Teddy Tinling, used to say 'Players dressed by me have an advantage over opponents,' and perhaps the number of Wimbledon champions among his clients proves him right. Think for a moment about how you respond to an opponent who truly 'looks the part'. Their appearance invariably diminishes your confidence. It is remarkable how much looking good can contribute to feeling good. So give some thought to your appearance in competition. Using the best quality equipment you can afford will move you another rung up the confidence ladder. Smart clothing and good quality equipment often form an integral part of the winning feeling which top class athletes describe.

CONFIDENCE IN THE CONDITIONS

Sometimes adverse weather conditions, or certain surfaces, or particular locations cause low self-confidence. This is usually related to previously unsuccessful performances in identical or similar circumstances. For instance, Ivan Lendl is not at his most confident on grass, and most golfers with a handicap of 18 do not relish playing when it's gusty. These prejudices may be based on logic (for example, 'clay courts are too slow for my serve and volley game'), on myth (for example, 'mud is the great equalizer in sport'), or on pure superstition (for example, 'that stadium is a jinx'). Whatever underlies the interpretation that conditions are unfavourable, the effect is always the same. Confidence is lowered. This in turn allows tenseness and anxiety to creep in and causes concentration to waver, which almost guarantees poor performance. Defeat will be blamed on the unfavourable conditions rather than the effects of lowered confidence. This reinforces the original negative attitude towards the conditions, which makes the problem even worse next time.

The solution is to change attitudes. One way to do this is by turning all your negative thoughts about the conditions into positive challenges. So, for instance, instead of thinking 'My approach shots miss the green 75 per cent of the time when it's raining,' say to yourself, 'My challenge is to improve on the 25 per cent of approach shots which land on the green when I play in the rain.' As you can see, there is no difference in the facts and the situation has not changed, you've just created a very different attitude. Giving yourself this realistic challenge enhances both motivation and confidence. Never underestimate how much attitude affects performance. Adopt a realistic but *positive* attitude.

CONFIDENCE AFTER INJURY

Any injury serious enough to prevent you from competing can be regarded as a threat to confidence. The after-effects of injury range from slight tentativeness which disappears the moment you get back into competition, to a genuine dread of further physical harm which stays with you long after the physical damage has healed. Often the effect is subtle and takes only the edge off one small part of your game, so that you might perhaps shy away from challenges. The danger is that this can spread to affect your general confidence. Choosing the most suitable strategy to recover confidence after injury depends upon how the injury occurred. Case study 2 deals with confidence shaken by an unpreventable accident.

Case study 2

Greg was a 6′ 8″ basketball player who suffered a badly twisted ankle while rebounding under the opposition basket. His foot landed on a team mate and his ankle turned over sharply. It was the sort of fluke accident that happens from time to time. Four weeks later his physiotherapist had confirmed that the ankle was fully recovered but Greg's confidence was still very shaky. He knew that there was little danger of the same thing happening again, but he was very reluctant to rebound. His attention was clearly divided between taking the ball cleanly and landing safely. Consequently his rebounding, which had once been a feature of his game, lost its effectiveness.

The strategy we used to overcome this problem was threefold. Firstly, Greg continued the strength rehabilitation programme set by his physiotherapist for an additional two weeks in order to rebuild his confidence in the strength of his ankle. Secondly, he used a combination of visualization and physical practice to gradually densensitize his fears about re-bounding.

Desensitization involves being exposed gradually to a situation which causes fear or concern and gaining confidence at each stage before moving on to the next. Fear is monitored numerically along the way. Greg was therefore instructed to visualize himself rebounding under specific conditions and to give an initial fear rating from one to ten. He was instructed to see and feel himself completing each rebound successfully for a few minutes and then give another fear rating. The process was repeated during physical practice.

Greg started by mentally rehearsing rebounding without opposition. Initially he rated this as a seven. After a few minutes' rehearsal, he felt more at ease with the situation and his rating had dropped to five. He then practised this physically for ten minutes after which time his fear rating was down to two. Greg progressed in this fashion over a period of five days until rebounding in a game situation had a fear rating of only two. The results of this programme are shown on page 99.

Desensitization programme to restore confidence

Mental practice	Rebounding alone	Rating: 7 down to 5
Physical practice	Rebounding alone	Rating: 2
Mental practice	Rebounding 1 on 1	Rating: 8 down to 5
Physical practice	Rebounding 1 on 1	Rating: 3
Mental practice	Rebounding 2 on 2	Rating: 6 down to 4
Physical practice	Rebounding 2 on 2	Rating: 3
Mental practice	Rebounding 3 on 3	Rating: 5 down to 3
Physical practice	Rebounding 3 on 3	Rating: 2
Mental practice	Rebounding 5 on 5	Rating: 5 down to 3
Physical practice	Rebounding 5 on 5	Rating: 2

To reinforce his growing confidence, Greg also devised positive self-statements related to this problem. During the first week he used 'It's getting stronger', which helped sustain his belief that the ankle was regaining strength. By the end of the second week this had developed into 'I'm flying again', which indicated that his positive attitude towards rebounding had returned in full and that the accident had been forgotten.

This strategy of desensitization is best for injuries sustained in circumstances beyond the control of the individual concerned. However, there is an alternative strategy which is effective when evasive action or an adjustment to technique could have prevented the original injury. This strategy can be referred to as 'Changing the script' which, as the name implies, involves visualizing the situation in which the injury was received but re-experiencing it with a different outcome. This technique was used by Ian in case study 1. Once the key to a different outcome is identified and the new 'script' is practised sufficiently, the memory of the original outcome becomes blurred and forgotten. The next exercise contains instructions for 'Changing the script'.

Changing the script

- Visualize the situation in which you were injured
- Replay the scene several times, noticing exactly what happened

- Identify the exact circumstances which caused the injury. What could you have done to change this outcome?

- Now rehearse the same situation but 'change the script' so that the outcome is different

- Continue rehearsing this new outcome until you feel confident of being able to cope with the original circumstances.

I hope that this chapter will have convinced you that confidence is not solely in the hands of the gods. *You* are the person responsible for determining how confident you feel in sport. To briefly review the general strategy for generating or restoring self-confidence, remember that if your confidence is heading on a downward spiral, **UPWARD** is the way to reverse the trend:

U   **Understand** exactly what has caused your confidence to fall.

P   **Personal images of confidence** Clarify exactly what confidence means to you.

W   **Winning feeling** Re-discover how it feels to be confident and successful and practice recreating the feeling.

A   **Action steps** Identify the barriers to renewed confidence.

R   **Routeplanner** Establish exactly how you will overcome each barrier and where that will take you.

D   **Decide** on the specific techniques for achieving these improvements to self-confidence.

Ideas for promoting confidence range from the simple principles of thorough preparation of the basics of your sport, to the techniques of desensitization and of 'changing the script'. In between, you have learnt how to change attitudes, how to act confidently, how to use positive self-statements and how to recreate the winning feeling. No book can hope to cover every eventuality in sport and it is up to you to take what you can from this chapter and adapt it to your own requirements. Remember that confidence is just as important as ability in sport, so be prepared to spend time finding the technique which halts your downward shift in confidence and puts you back on the upward spiral.

ANXIETY: THE ENEMY WITHIN

To the psychologist, anxiety is 'a complex emotional state'. To the public, it is a feeling synonymous with worry, tension, apprehension or fear. To the athlete it is public enemy number one. When a competitor 'freezes' in the big moment or commits an inexplicable blunder, anxiety is very often the root cause. When Steve Davis missed a routine pot on the final black of the final frame to lose the 1985 World Professional Snooker Championship to Dennis Taylor, the only possible explanation was that 'the pressure got to him'. Imagine the isolation of that moment. Even as a spectator, the tension was unbearable.

Sport is littered with the broken dreams of sportsmen and women who cracked like eggs when they most needed calm. Penalty shoot-outs in major soccer competitions are heart-stopping moments for all concerned, and the burden of responsibility on individual players often results in spectacular misses by players who are unable to handle the pressure.

Unfortunately, too many athletes accept anxiety as an inevitable part of the total sporting experience. What is your reaction when, having been on the verge of triumph, you allow anxiety to snatch victory and hand it to your opponent on a plate? Do you shrug your shoulders and hope it doesn't happen again, or do you resolve to do something about it? Perhaps, finally, a solution may be at hand.

WHAT IS ANXIETY?

The nature of sport is to place *stress* upon those who take part, to make demands upon their physical and mental energies. Sport

Steve Davies

The basic cause of anxiety

The perceived demands of the task
outweigh belief in ability

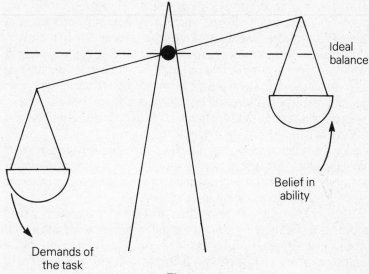

Fig 5.1

offers its participants an opportunity for growth, a chance to push back personal boundaries, to liberate the body and the mind simultaneously. In itself there is nothing damaging about this stress. In fact quite the contrary; stress can be a positive influence, what we might call the 'challenge' in life.

At the same time as providing challenge, sport also provides uncertainty. The outcome of any sporting action, the result of any sporting contest, always carries some doubt. At the precise moment the archer fires an arrow, or the golfer swings a club, the outcome is unknown. The stress which sport provides, therefore, is inevitably cloaked in uncertainty. This combination of stress and uncertainty is the potential villain of the piece because it can be interpreted either as a blessing or as a threat. While one person may be motivated by the challenge and will relish the uncertainty, another may be distressed by it and become anxious.

Anxiety is simply a reflection of uncertainty. It is an emotional response characterized by feelings of worry and tension which, in sport, is brought on by doubts – doubts about the outcome, doubts about ourselves, doubts about safety, doubts about what others will think. Unfortunately for athletes, the human mind harbours more demons than a Stephen Spielberg film.

Much of life is spent 'weighing up' situations, comparing the demands of a task with what we believe ourselves capable of. However, as fig. 5.1 shows, an imbalance in our perception of these things is the fundamental cause of anxiety.

For instance, when skiers look down from the top of a difficult run, they compare the demands of the hill with what they believe they can cope with. If a skier is convinced that the run is within his or her capabilities, there will be no anxiety. If, on the other hand, the skier has some doubt, then the hill appears threatening and anxiety is the result.

The fact that anxiety is dependent upon the *perceptions* of an individual makes it a very personal and unpredictable problem. It will occur if either the perceived demands of the task increase or belief in ability declines for some reason.

Anxiety may be no more than a fleeting moment of dread when, as a cricketer, you find yourself under another high catch, having just dropped a previous one, or it may develop into a long-term aversion towards particular situations, such as a fear of facing pace bowlers after a series of failures. In either case, self-belief has been shaken and has tipped the balance towards anxiety, although the actual demands of the task remain the same.

As self-belief declines, so the perceived demands of the task grow in equal measure. When things are going badly the task appears progressively more demanding. Targets appear to shrink and events speed up. In such circumstances rational thought often proves impossible and instincts tend to take over. The effect upon performance, especially where fine muscle control and a clear head are essential, often proves disastrous.

WHAT CONTRIBUTES TO ANXIETY?

Sport presents a vast array of stressors for an athlete to cope with. At different times the body may have to compete in the face of excessive heat, humidity, or in freezing cold, thick mud, in fatigue, illness and even injury. These physical stressors have a profound but predictable influence on sports performance, either by making the task more difficult to perform efficiently, or by planting doubt in the performer's mind that they are equal to the challenge.

In addition, there are several stressors of a psychological nature which have a more subtle, but equally real, impact on performance. It is worth discussing these one by one.

The importance of the event

The more important the contest the greater the stress, and the more likely the competitor is to become anxious. Clearly, the final of an important tournament is more stressful than a pre-season friendly. Studies have shown that in national championships as many as 67 per cent of competitors experience anxiety symptoms, and in Olympic finals this can rise to almost 100 per cent.

Remember, though, that 'importance' is a relative term which depends primarily upon how the individual views the situation. For example, even a seasoned professional can become nervous before a comeback performance following injury. Doubts about whether the old skills will still be there, or whether the injury is fully healed, can make the occasion seem more important than a cup final in the eyes of the player.

The size and the supportiveness of the crowd

An audience can make an incredible difference. The presence of even a single person can influence performance, either positively, by increasing your motivation, or adversely, by getting you flustered. This effect is based upon an awareness that onlookers evaluate performers, and a basic human fear of being evaluated unfavourably.

Generally, the effect on performance is exaggerated one way or the other by a large audience, so that a crowd of many thousands has the potential to bring out the very best in you or to paralyse you with fear. The supportiveness of those watching is also a factor, and this accounts for the significant home advantage in many sports, especially professional soccer. Research has shown that a supportive crowd tends to reduce the anxiety and increase the motivation of performers, whereas a hostile crowd makes anxiety more likely and often increases aggressive behaviour.

A situation particularly likely to cause anxiety occurs when a previously supportive crowd suddenly turns against you, or even if you just *believe* that an audience has started to judge you unfavourably. But as a general rule, audiences prove more disruptive to the performance of novice players than to experienced or highly skilled performers.

An emphasis on the individual

Participants in individual sports have been shown to suffer more anxiety before, during and after competition than participants in team sports. This is because the sense of isolation and exposure is much greater in individual sports like skating, gymnastics, tennis and golf than in the relative anonymity of team sports. However, there are some moments in team sports when one individual is stressed more than his or her team mates by being put momentarily in the spotlight. The batsman in cricket, the shooter in netball, and the player who takes a penalty in hockey or soccer are all faced with moments of isolation when their individual contribution is placed under close scrutiny.

During the brief spells when a player actually has possession of the ball or puck they are, in essence, solo performers and their contribution is judged by opponents and team mates alike. Many performers become acutely aware of this fact and feel threatened by it. In these situations, anxiety may show itself in many ways; an unwillingness to shoot for goal, a tendency to get rid of the ball quickly, or habitually attempting too much.

The fear of physical injury

For the recreational skier the possibility of getting hurt can be a genuine source of anxiety. Typically this anxiety causes important changes in technique. Anxious skiers will often lean back too far, or tense their legs, or crouch down, any of which may result in the fall that they fear.

However, even in those sports which do carry an obvious risk of physical injury, athletes in competition tend to become more anxious about not performing well than they do about injuring themselves. In apparently high-risk sports such as bobsleigh, the threat of being assessed unfavourably by others or of letting oneself down far outweighs any fear of getting hurt. Keith Power, a member of the British four-man bobsleigh team expressed it like this:

> The risk of being injured is real but remote. The risk of making a complete idiot of yourself is ever present and much more frightening.

The expectations of success

The stress upon competitors is probably at its greatest when they are favourites to win. Anxiety almost certainly contributed to Tom McKean's poor showing in the final of the 800 metres in the 1987 World Athletic Championships, because his form in the qualifying rounds of the Rome competition had made him a genuine gold medal contender. The press and the general public had proclaimed him a natural successor to Britain's golden trio of middle distance runners: Steve Cram, Sebastian Coe and Steve Ovett. Expectations soared and the pressure grew accordingly.

In these situations it is easy for a performer to magnify the task ahead. The hopes of a nation weigh far more heavily on a young man's shoulders than his own hopes and dreams. The race itself was a disaster. McKean's nervous performance had all the hallmarks of 'energy left on the warm-up track'. He seemed to lack the spring in his stride that had been so evident in earlier races. He got himself boxed in, became indecisive about making a move, and allowed his attention to become focused on the runner immediately in front of him. As a result McKean was in no position at all to counter the winning surge of Kenya's Billy Konchella and trailed in last.

Unfortunately it is not only World Championships which cause this reaction. During any contest in which you sense a pressure to win there is a potential threat to your self-esteem. Athletes are only too aware that many people have invested time, effort and money into their preparation. They may feel that the only way to repay this debt of gratitude to coaches, family and perhaps sponsors is to win. Consequently, some athletes compete with a great burden of self-inflicted pressure upon them, having set totally unrealistic goals for themselves.

Tom McKean

When you add all these factors together you will see that there can be many anxious moments in sport. For so many athletes, anxiety acts as the enemy within, the opponent who ruins performance. And yet, clearly, sport ought to contain some element of stress. Sport would not be sport if the challenge wasn't there. There has to be some pressure, but the key question is, 'How much?'

RESPONDING TO STRESS

It should be clear by now that stress can either be the force which stirs you into action or a burden which inhibits you. The determining factor is not so much the *amount* of stress but your *response* to it. In fact, it could be said that stress results in two closely related but separate responses, a physical one and a psychological one.

The physical response

Whenever the body is stressed in any way an automatic physical response occurs which prepares it for action. Typically we experience a rush of adrenalin, breathing quickens and the heart beats faster. This general activation of the body is referred to as the preparation for 'fight or flight', and is an instinctive response to challenge. As a result the body becomes more alert, better prepared to react and feels less pain. This is what you might call getting 'psyched up' and what psychologists refer to as becoming physiologically aroused.

As athletes come to realize through experience, and as research has confirmed, there is a relationship between the arousal level of an athlete and the quality of his or her performance. Generally, as arousal increases, performance levels also tend to increase until an optimum point of arousal is reached, beyond which further increases in arousal can cause performance to deteriorate dramatically. In other words, the trick is to become sufficiently 'psyched up' without becoming 'psyched out'. This relationship between performance and arousal level is presented in the graph in fig. 5.2. It is wrong to believe that the more psyched up you get the better you will perform. You will need to discover your optimum level of arousal, that is, the amount

The relationship between quality of performance in sport and level of arousal

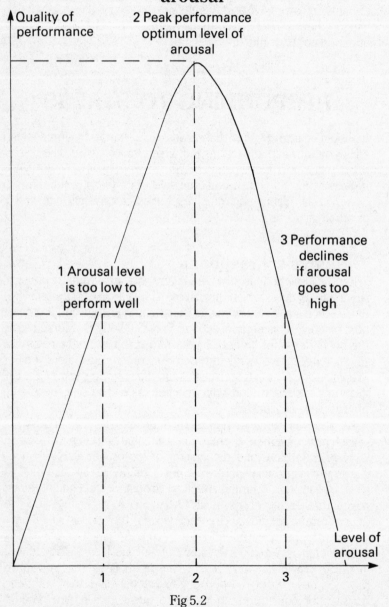

Fig 5.2

of stress needed to produce the best performance. This optimum level varies greatly from person to person and from task to task.

Peak performance in explosive activities, such as weightlifting, requires higher levels of physiological arousal than in manipulative tasks involving fine muscle control, such as snooker. It is obvious that you would need to psych up for weightlifting and stay calm for snooker. But what about the sports in between these two extremes? What is the correct level of arousal for netball or soccer or cricket or tennis? Here it becomes much more difficult to generalize.

If you have ever witnessed a team psych-up taking place before a rugby match you will know just how ritualistic and tribal psychological preparation can be. The stomping and the chanting and the overt aggression which occurs in rugby changing rooms up and down the country on a Saturday afternoon is designed to raise arousal levels to fever pitch in preparation for the 'battle' ahead. The underlying assumption is that all rugby players require a high level of arousal to perform at their best. For many players this is a valid assumption and a fervent warm up may prove extremely effective. Sometimes, though, the arousal level achieved does not match the requirements of the specific tasks to be performed nor the needs of the individual players. For instance, in rugby, the outside half performs a role which requires vision and judgement, and consequently great outside halfs like Jonathan Davies and John Rutherford tend to be the most relaxed players on the field. The excitement and aggression which might benefit a flanker or a prop forward would almost certainly diminish their ability to make considered decisions.

Optimum arousal depends to an even greater extent on the sort of person you are. For instance, Dean Richards, the English rugby team's number eight forward, whose playing position *theoretically* demands a high level of physiological arousal, illustrated the very personal nature of pre-match preparation when he said, 'I'm not one of nature's headbangers. I don't need all that macho mayhem to get myself prepared.'

It is clear that some people are at their best when excited and agitated while others need to remain calm in order to perform well. Ultimately, the only reliable means of determining your own optimum arousal level is to use some means of monitoring performance levels in relation to emotional state. In the final chapter, as part of the programme for total preparation, there is a performance diary which shows you how to record details of arousal level in relation to the quality of your sports performance.

The psychological response

Arousal of the body happens automatically when it is stressed, and this is accompanied by a more complex psychological response which may cause further arousal. The psychological response is based on an evaluation of whatever is causing the stress. If your imagination moves into overdrive and you start to have doubts about whether the challenge is within your capabilities, then arousal may be pushed way beyond its optimum point, causing many unwanted symptoms. This process is shown in fig. 5.3. Notice that it is the anxiety caused by an unfavourable evaluation of the stressor which causes the harm. The physical activation of the body only becomes a problem when it is pushed too high.

The relationship between stress, arousal and anxiety

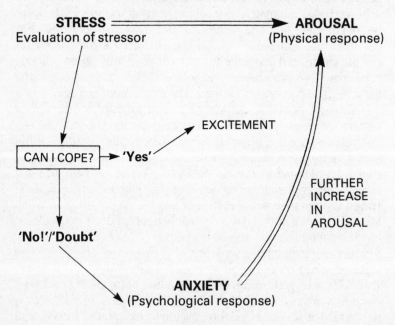

Fig 5.3

Ideally a performer should be aroused to the optimum level but not be in the least bit anxious. As an athlete you must aim to reap the benefits of heightened arousal without allowing anxiety to push it too high. This requires you to understand your own natural inclinations and to be sensitive to your body signals. Learning to handle the stresses of competition involves learning to read your physical responses and to develop the skills necessary to keep anxiety at bay.

INDIVIDUAL DIFFERENCES IN ANXIETY

Anxiety is experienced by most people from time to time, but it is quite clear that some people are much more prone to becoming anxious than others. This potential for anxiety is considered to be a part of personality and will therefore not disappear overnight. Psychologists call the tendency to become anxious, *trait anxiety* in order to distinguish it from the anxiety response itself, which is called *state anxiety*. This is not to say that those individuals who are high in trait anxiety are constantly in a nervous, tense condition, just that they experience the symptoms of anxiety more often and more intensely.

It is impossible to predict exactly what circumstances will trigger off anxiety. Some individuals thrive in situations which would terrify others. A seat in the dentist's chair, for instance, produces very diverse responses from different people, and similarly while some individuals are reduced to nervous wrecks at the mere thought of speaking in public, others take such occasions in their stride. Even seemingly innocuous tasks such as being introduced to a perfect stranger can generate anxiety in some people, the intensity of which many others would find hard to comprehend.

There is no evidence to suggest that athletes high in trait anxiety are any less likely to become champions, although clearly they do have a greater need to develop ways of avoiding the negative effects of anxiety during performance.

Research has shown that older and more experienced athletes have less anxiety about competition. There are two possible explanations for this. Either it is because sportspeople learn to cope effectively with the stresses of competition, or perhaps it is

The sports competition anxiety test

Below are some statements about how people feel when they compete in sports and games. Read each statement and decide if you feel this way hardly ever (**A**), sometimes (**B**) or often (**C**) when you compete. There are no right and wrong answers. Do not spend too much time on any one statement, and do not look at the scoring instructions until you have completed the test.

		A	B	C
1	Competing against others is socially enjoyable	☐	☐	☐
2	Before I compete I feel uneasy	☐	☐	☐
3	Before I compete I worry about not performing well	☐	☐	☐
4	I am a good sportsman when I compete	☐	☐	☐
5	When I compete I worry about making mistakes	☐	☐	☐
6	Before I compete I am calm	☐	☐	☐
7	Setting a goal is important when competing	☐	☐	☐
8	Before I compete I get a queasy feeling in my stomach	☐	☐	☐
9	Just before competing I notice my heart beats faster than usual	☐	☐	☐
10	I like to compete in games that demand considerable physical energy	☐	☐	☐
11	Before I compete I feel relaxed	☐	☐	☐
12	Before I compete I am nervous	☐	☐	☐
13	Team sports are more exciting than individual sports	☐	☐	☐
14	I get nervous waiting to start the contest	☐	☐	☐
15	Before I compete I usually get uptight	☐	☐	☐

Exercise 10

that highly anxious athletes drop out of sport because competition is too unpleasant for them. The true explanation is probably that both forces are in operation.

However, assuming that you have no wish to drop out, then you must find a solution to competition anxiety. As always, the first step towards resolving problems is self-analysis. Exercise 10 is the Sports competition anxiety test (Martens, 1977) which enables you to assess your own tendency towards anxiety during sports competitions.

How to calculate your score

For questions numbered 2, 3, 5, 8, 9, 12, 14 and 15:

$$A = 1; \quad B = 2; \quad C = 3$$

For questions numbered 6 and 11:

$$A = 3; \quad B = 2; \quad C = 1$$

Ignore your answers for questions numbered 1, 4, 7, 10, and 13.

Add up all your scores to give a total of between 10 and 30. The higher your score the more prone you are to anxiety during competition. Using the following table, compare your score with those of other sportsmen and sportswomen. The scores indicate the percentage of males and females who are *less* anxious (or *as* anxious) than you about sports competition. For example, if you scored 21 on the test, 69 per cent of males and 42 per cent of females are as anxious or less anxious about sports competition than you are.

Remember that the ideal state for the sports performer is one of mental alertness and physical relaxation. Those who are not at all anxious may be insufficiently aroused by competition to reach optimum alertness, whereas those who become very anxious may lose all physical relaxation.

LEARNING TO RECOGNIZE ANXIETY

Anxiety can be recognized on three levels: by physical responses (*somatic* level), by particular thought processes (*cognitive* level),

Sports competition anxiety test
Normal scores for male and female adults

| | Percentages | |
Score	Males	Females
30	99	99
29	99	93
28	97	88
27	93	82
26	89	75
25	86	65
24	82	59
23	78	53
22	74	47
21	69	42
20	61	35
19	50	28
18	40	22
17	30	15
16	24	10
15	18	8
14	14	6
13	9	4
12	7	3
11	5	2
10	1	1

or by specific patterns of behaviour (*behavioural* level). The following table lists some of the symptoms on each level. Use this as a reference for recognizing anxiety. As you can see, many of the somatic responses are only too obvious, but not all of them are a cause for concern. Increases in heart rate, respiration and adrenalin production are positive influences on performance, but the appearance of further somatic symptoms, and the emergence of the cognitive responses listed, means that excitement has turned to anxiety and remedial action is required.

Symptoms of anxiety

Cognitive
Indecisiveness
Mental confusion
Feeling heavy
Negative thoughts
Poor concentration
Irritability
Fear
Forgetfulness
Loss of confidence

Somatic
Increased blood
  pressure
Pounding heart
Increased respira-
  tory rate
Sweating
Clammy hands and
  feet
Butterflies in the
  stomach
Increased adrenalin
Dry mouth
Wanting to go to
  the toilet
Muscular tension
Ringing in the ears
Tightness in the
  neck and
  shoulders
Trembling
Blushing
Distorted vision
Twitching
Yawning a lot
Voice distortion
Feeling weak
Nausea
Vomiting
Diarrhoea
Loss of appetite
Sleeplessness

Behavioural
Biting fingernails
Lethargic move-
  ments
Playing safe
Inhibited posture
Going through the
  motions
Introversion
Uncharacteristic
  displays of
  extroversion

LEARNING TO CONTROL ANXIETY

It is often said that pressure focuses the mind. This is all well and good so long as the pressure does not tense the body unnecessarily. To perform at your best you need just the right amount of tension in the body. Too much will result in poor muscular control.

All skilled movement involves controlling which muscles are tensed and which ones are relaxed. For example, as you tense your biceps the muscle fibres contract so that your arm bends. To straighten your arm you tense the opposite muscle, the triceps. To hold your arm in a particular position requires you to balance the tension in the two muscle groups. This pairing of muscles occurs throughout the body so that all bodily positions are achieved through the delicate balance of tension and relaxation in each pair of muscles.

During movement the voluntary contraction of one muscle automatically causes its opposite muscle to relax. However, if a muscle contracts involuntarily, due to anxiety, the opposite muscle will also contract to maintain the equilibrium of the body. This means that severe muscular tension can build up simply by worrying. Unfortunately, the tension may go undetected until it brings about poor performance because movement has become rigid and awkward. If you have ever attempted delicate skills immediately after a heavy weight training session, you will know how much excessive muscle tension interferes with fine muscle control.

Edwin Moses

To an extent, movement counteracts muscular tension, which is why many athletes prefer to stay mobile just prior to the start of competition. In addition, there are several relaxation techniques which can complement a warm-up routine, or be used the night before competition to ensure a good night's sleep, or during competition to ward off unwanted tension before it appears. Relaxation forms the basis of anxiety control. It can be defined as 'an absence of tension'. So, if you learn to induce relaxation at will, then the major negative symptom of anxiety will be banished at a stroke.

Some people are more suited to one type of relaxation technique than others, so the only reliable strategy for discovering which one is most effective for you is to try a variety of techniques. Three methods of relaxation are described in this chapter, which are referred to as progressive muscular relaxation, the quiet place, and the five breath technique. I cannot emphasize strongly enough that none of these techniques is likely to be effective immediately. Like any new skill, they require practice and patience. You must remember that there is nothing inherently good about relaxation. It is an effective remedy for *excess* tension but once your ideal state of arousal is reached, further relaxation could leave you too docile.

PROGRESSIVE MUSCULAR RELAXATION

This technique was developed in the 1930s by Dr Edmund Jacobson and athletes sometimes refer to a progressive muscular relaxation (PMR) session as 'doing a Jacobson'. The technique involves progressing from one muscle group to the next, alternately creating and releasing tension. This makes you much more sensitive to when and where tension is present in the body. In effect, PMR trains the body to identify tension and to release it automatically.

Becoming proficient in this technique takes time and requires effort, but the ability to induce deep relaxation has many benefits. While you are learning PMR it is necessary to generate the tension artificially by voluntarily contracting specific muscle groups. This is how you begin to recognize *where* you are tense. At the same time your body becomes used to relaxing the contraction, thereby releasing the tension. Initially PMR is a long and thorough process but once you become tuned in to your body relaxing tense muscles it becomes automatic, and is a way of introducing flow back into your movement.

This exercise is far too long for you to memorize, so either ask a friend to read out the instructions in a quiet, relaxed voice or record them yourself on to a cassette. You may find that neither solution is really satisfactory. If so, a cassette tape containing this and other relaxation exercises is available from Performance Management Associates, 116 Bower Street, Bedford.

At first you should spend about 20 or 30 minutes on each PMR session, but gradually, as you become more proficient, this time can be reduced.

Sit comfortably or lie down with your eyes closed. Relax your arms by your sides and don't cross your legs. As you follow the instructions, you will focus on the word *relax*, but do not try to force the relaxation, just let it happen. Don't worry about how well you are doing, simply let the relaxation flow over you and let it deepen at its own pace.

Keep your breathing steady and shallow. Notice how, when you breathe out, you relax a little more. Breathe in and out through your nose and each time you breathe out relax a little more.

Don't hold your breath. Keep your breathing steady and regular, and concentrate on the word *relax* each time you breathe out. Now we will go through the muscle groups one by one so that you can feel the difference between tension and relaxation.

First your *hands and forearms*. Tense these muscles by clenching your fists as tightly as you can. Clench your fists tightly. Feel the tension in your hands and forearms . . . and now relax. Relax your hands and forearms and notice the difference between tension and relaxation.

Focus on the word *relax* while letting the muscles in your hands and forearms unwind more and more deeply. Concentrate on the feeling of letting go.

Now tense the muscles in the front of your upper arm – the *biceps*. Tense these by bending your arms at the elbow and trying to touch your shoulders with your wrists. Tense the biceps tight. Feel the tension in your biceps . . . and now relax. Let your arms fall back by your sides and notice the difference between tension and relaxation in your biceps.

Focus on the word *relax* while letting your bicep muscles loosen and unwind more and more deeply. Continue the feeling of letting go as the muscles unwind and relax.

Now tense the muscles in the back of your upper arms – the *triceps*. Tense these by straightening your arms as hard as you can so that they feel like blocks of wood. Straighten your arms . . . hard . . . harder. Feel the tension in your triceps. Now relax. As you let go of the tension, concentrate on the word *relax*, and allow the feeling of relaxation to spread throughout your arms.

Now tense the muscles in your *shoulders*. Shrug your shoulders by drawing them up into your neck as tightly as you can. Shrug them tightly. Feel the tension in your shoulders. Hold it . . . and relax. Let your shoulders drop and feel the tension ease away. As your muscles unwind, concentrate on the word *relax*.

Now tense the muscles in your *neck*. Tense the muscles as hard as you can so that your neck feels like stone. Feel the tension and hold it . . . tightly . . . and relax. Let your head rest back gently on your shoulders . . . no effort . . . no tension . . . and notice the difference between tension and relaxation. Focus on the word *relax* as the muscles in your neck unwind more and more. Let go of the tension . . . and relax.

Now tense the muscles in your *forehead*. Raise your eyebrows as high as you can and feel the tension in your forehead. Feel the tension and hold it . . . hold it . . . and now relax. Let your eyebrows drop. Let the tension go from your forehead and focus on the word *relax*.

Now tense the muscles in your *eyebrows and eyelids*. Frown as hard as you can and squeeze your eyes tightly shut. Feel the tension . . . hold it . . . hold it . . . and relax. Smooth out your brow, relax your eyelids, keep your eyes still and gaze straight ahead. Notice the difference between the feelings of tension and relaxation around your eyes and focus on the word *relax* as the muscles around your eyes unwind more and more deeply.

Now tense the muscles in your *jaw*. Bite your teeth together as tightly as you can . . . tight . . . tighter . . . feel the tension in your jaw . . . feel the tension . . . and relax. Part your teeth slightly so there is no pressure and feel the difference between tension and relaxation in your jaw. Feel the relief of letting go of the tension. Relax your jaw more and more deeply and focus on the word *relax*.

Now tense the muscles in your *tongue and throat*. Put the tip of your tongue against the roof of your mouth and push up as hard as you can. Press up hard. . . harder. . . feel the tension in your tongue and throat . . . and relax. Let your tongue drop to the bottom of your mouth, still and relaxed and feel the tension ease away from your tongue and throat. Continue the feeling of letting go while you focus on the word *relax*.

Now tense the muscles in your *lips and face*. Press your lips together as tightly as you can. Press them together tight . . . tighter . . . feel the tension in your lips and face . . . and relax. Relax your lips and allow your face to sag. Feel the muscles unwind more and more. Let go of the tension as you focus on the word *relax*.

Now tense the muscles in your *chest*. Take a deep breath so that your chest tenses like a bodybuilder. Hold it tightly. Feel the tension in your chest and hold it . . . and relax. Breathe right out and feel the relief of letting go. Keep your breathing shallow. Every time you breathe out notice how you relax a little more. Focus on the word *relax* as your chest unwinds more and more.

Now tense the muscles in your *stomach*. Push down into your stomach as though preparing to be punched. Make your stomach muscles hard and rigid like a washboard. Hold the tension . . . hold it . . . and relax. Let the muscles loosen and unwind. Notice the difference between tension and relaxation in your stomach. Focus on the word *relax* as the feeling of relaxation spreads.

Now tense the muscles in your *hips and lower back*. Sit ramrod straight and tense your buttocks and your hips tightly . . . tighter . . . feel the tension . . . and relax. Let all the tension fall away from your hips and your lower back. Notice how it feels to let go of the tension. As the muscles unwind focus on the word *relax*.

Now tense the muscles in your *legs*. Pull your toes up tightly so that your thighs tense like treetrunks and your calf muscles become hard. Hold the tension in your legs . . . tight . . . tighter . . . and relax. Let your legs loosen and unwind as the tension falls away. Notice the difference between tension and relaxation in your legs. Focus on the word *relax* as the muscles unwind deeper and deeper.

Now let the feeling of relaxation spread right through your whole body. Keep your breathing regular and relaxed and every time you breathe out relax a little more. Let the relaxation flow over you. Feel as though you are sinking more and more. You are calm and deeply relaxed and there is no tension. Focus on the word *relax* and enjoy the feeling.

THE QUIET PLACE

The last relaxation technique worked on the principle that relaxation in the muscles creates a sense of well-being in the mind. There are, however, several techniques which work in the opposite direction whereby passive, relaxed thought in the mind spreads relaxation throughout the body. One such technique, popularized by John Syer and Chris Connolly of the Sporting Bodymind organization, is known as 'The quiet place' and involves visualizing a real or imaginary location which carries strong associations of relaxation.

As with all relaxation techniques, make no attempt to force yourself to relax. This is counter productive. Learn to just let it happen so that there will be no distracting or unwanted thoughts.

The quiet place is a visualization exercise designed to transport you from any stressful situation to a place where you will feel relaxed by what is going on around you. You first need to think of a place that is special to you, a place that you associate with feelings of peace and quiet, and where you can really take things easy. Practise this technique in a place where you will not be disturbed. Sit or lie down, close your eyes and take a few deep breaths, exhaling very slowly, before you start the exercise.

Imagine yourself alone and undisturbed in your favourite quiet place. It can be anywhere you wish, by the sea, in a forest or high in the mountains; any place where you feel peaceful and relaxed.

Now become very aware of the place and yourself in it. Notice what you are wearing, how you are sitting or lying and how relaxed you feel. Look around you; notice the scenery, the colours, the smells and the sounds. What season is it? What time of day? What does the ground by your side feel like to touch?

Recall all the little features of the place which signify its peacefulness. It may be the sound of birds, the warmth of the sun or the rustle of leaves. Immerse yourself in the feel of this place where you relax completely and enjoy the sensation.

Now without opening your eyes bring your attention back to the room you are sitting in and very gently squeeze your left thumb with the fingers of your right hand. As you do, allow yourself to drift back to your quiet place and immerse yourself in it once more. Notice all the little details of your quiet place and again feel totally relaxed and at ease.

Repeat the process of allowing the scene to fade and then squeeze your thumb once more to return to the quiet place. Do this another two or three times before releasing your thumb and opening your eyes.

After sufficient practice, holding your thumb will act as a 'trigger' that will take you to your peaceful little hideaway immediately you feel the need to relax. It can become an effective method of staying calm before competition or during extended breaks in the action.

THE FIVE BREATH TECHNIQUE

Another effective method of relaxing involves focusing attention exclusively upon the rhythm of your breathing. The five breath technique, described below, is a mild form of self-hypnosis which removes tension and clears the mind. Once mastered, this technique will help you relax very quickly indeed. It can be used any time you feel yourself tensing up and will be effective even in highly charged situations.

First though, you will need to spend time perfecting the technique. This is best done in quiet surroundings where you will not be disturbed. Just five minutes a day practising should enable you to relax at will in about four to six weeks. Again you will need either to ask a friend to read the instructions slowly and clearly, or obtain the cassette recommended on page 120.

Lie or sit comfortably, eyes closed, arms by your side.
Take a deep breath. Concentrate on allowing the muscles of your face and your neck to relax as you breathe out.
Take a second deep breath. Allow the muscles in your

shoulders and arms to relax as you breathe out.

Take a third deep breath. Allow the muscles in your chest, stomach and back to relax as you breathe out.

Take a fourth deep breath. Allow your legs and feet to relax as you breathe out.

Take a fifth deep breath and focus on relaxing your whole body as you breathe out.

Because you are in 'hypnotic time' you may stay in this state of relaxation for as long as you like, although in real time it will only be for five minutes. At the end of that period you will know that it is time to return to full consciousness.

When you wish to become fully conscious count slowly down from five to one telling yourself that you will feel as relaxed and alert as you wish to be for the task at hand. This sense of calmness and alertness will remain with you when you revive.

KEEP WINNING IN PERSPECTIVE

Learning to relax is a major factor in coping with competition stress. But there are many other things you can do which will deflect the pressure. For a start, keep winning in its proper perspective. Sport induces fear and tension because it is so important to its devotees. It arouses extremes of passion which few other activities can match. For some, sport seems to be as important as life and death itself, while for a few it is, as the late Bill Shankly once said, 'much more important than that'.

No matter how desperately you want to win, it is not your self-esteem which is on the line if you fail. If you believe that you will be a lesser person if the result goes against you, you are condemning yourself to a career riddled with anxiety, a career which never quite fulfils its true potential. By all means hate to lose, but don't hate yourself if you do. A simple acknowledgement that your best is the most you can hope to give will, ironically, mean that winning seems that much easier.

Setting realistic goals for yourself is another way to help you measure success. Your ultimate goal will always revolve around being a winner, but your intermediate goals should relate to effort and long-term development rather than victory. Focus on controlling the controllable and you will be surprised how much less pressure you feel.

Hopefully by now you will understand the process which causes anxiety and can see ways to prevent it disrupting your perform-ance. It would be impossible to describe methods of coping with *every* eventuality in sport, so I have tried to use examples which will be recognizable to the majority of athletes. The challenge for you now is to mould what you have learned to your particular needs. The skills required to stop anxiety spoiling performance can be summarized as follows:

- Relaxation
- Self-esteem that is not measured in terms of victories or defeats
- Realistic goals

The message I have tried to convey is that the major problem in competition is letting your mind work against you. The mental skills described in this chapter and throughout the book will help your mind and your body become a more effective partnership, but be patient with yourself. Learning to release your true potential takes time and perseverance.

THE ART OF CONCENTRATION

Concentration is a precious commodity. Coaches plead with their players to keep it, while defeated athletes explain sadly how they lost theirs. The whole sporting fraternity listens sympathetically and gives a nod of recognition. It has happened to us all.

But what exactly does happen during this phenomenon we call 'losing concentration'? To answer this question in a meaningful way, it is first necessary to explore the nature of concentration. Generally speaking, concentration refers to the fixing of attention; and attention, as every naughty schoolboy knows, is what the teacher asks for when you are quite happily daydreaming. This will cause schoolchildren, once rebuked, to sit bolt upright and hang on the teacher's every word, and that demonstrates the basic ability we all have to exert conscious control over concentration when required to do so.

Concentration, therefore, should be thought of as the process of controlling attention so that all thoughts and senses are focused totally upon a selected object or activity to the exclusion of everything else. Good concentration is simply keeping attention fixed on the right thing at the right time, and 'lost' concentration is when the focus of attention becomes less than total or when it shifts to other things.

An important step towards mastering the art of concentration is to understand the different dimensions of attention. The first important fact to remember is that attention involves selectivity. Sadly for us, the human central nervous system is simply not capable of processing the enormous quantity of sensory information which is available at any moment in time, and so we are forced to filter out most of it. The nervous system handles the job of identifying information to be processed, and once our

Javed Miandad

concentration capacity is reached nothing else will be noticed. This is not always a conscious process and when we are day-dreaming, for instance, our entire concentration capacity may be filled with internal thoughts so that we notice almost nothing going on around us.

Fortunately, most people are quite able to consciously redirect attention as and when required, although, having said that, very many simple errors in sport are caused by attention being directed inappropriately. For instance, when a star cricketer like Pakistan's Javed Miandad takes the crease to bat, his concentration processes play a prime role. The virtuoso strokes he produces are only possible through the effective use of several

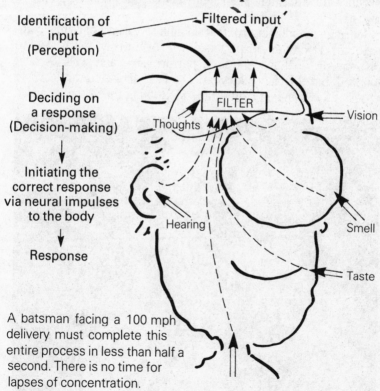

How sensory input competes for concentration capacity

Identification of input (Perception)

Deciding on a response (Decision-making)

Initiating the correct response via neural impulses to the body

Response

FILTER

Filtered input

Thoughts

Vision

Hearing

Smell

Taste

A batsman facing a 100 mph delivery must complete this entire process in less than half a second. There is no time for lapses of concentration.

Fig 6.1

different sensory systems: *vision* to perceive the speed, position and swing of the ball; *hearing* the subtle changes of spin; and a delicate sense of *feel*, which permits accurate repositioning of the bat and body in unison.

Although these sensory systems function in a very complex way, the underlying principle of selective attention which some performers have mastered while others struggle, is a very simple one. Fig 6.1 shows how sensory input competes for our attention and outlines the process by which skills are then produced.

If Javed Miandad wasted his valuable concentration capacity attending to the noise or movement of the crowd, he would become less aware of the important details which aid successful batting. In a sport where facing a 100 mph delivery leaves less than half a second to identify sensory input, decide on which stroke to play, and initiate the necessary bodily movements to produce the shot, any inefficiency in concentration would prove disastrous.

During any sporting contest an infinite variety of things compete for attention. Experience will eventually teach you to distinguish what is central to performance and what is best ignored, but this may take years. You can short-cut this learning process by spending a little time identifying those things which

Greg Whyte

Key details and distractions
(example)

Name: <u>Greg Whyte</u>   Sport: <u>Pistol shooting</u>

Key details	Distractions
1 The target	1 My own thoughts
2 The gun sight	2 Wind changes
3 Finger pressure on trigger	3 Other competiton
4	4 Background noise
5	5
6	6
7	7
8	8
9	9
10	10

Key details and distractions

Name: _____   Sport: _____

Key details	Distractions
1	1
2	2
3	3
4	4
5	5
6	6
7	7
8	8
9	9
10	10

Exercise 11

are indispensable to performance and those which are potential distractions. In exercise 11 you should try to identify the key details and common distractions in your sport. To guide you, I have listed the key details and distractions for a pistol shooter.

Many things can happen to drag your attention from the relevant to the irrelevant. Excitement, elation, anxiety, self-doubt, dispute or anger, and a host of other emotions, can all cause attention to wander no matter how hard you try to guard against it. Inevitably, when attention is diverted away from the action, performance suffers, so learning how to overcome distractions is crucial.

Identifying key performance details moves you one step closer to perfect concentration, but there is still a long way to go. A second important fact to remember about attention is that, in addition to the selectivity dimension, it has direction and width as well. At any moment, your attention can be directed either externally towards objects outside your body, such as this book, or internally on your own thoughts and feelings. Also, your attention can have either a narrow focus, where you concentrate intently on a specific object or thought, or a broad focus where you are aware of many things at once.

The two dimensions of direction and width are independent of one another and this results in four distinct attentional styles: broad-external, narrow-external, broad-internal, and narrow-internal. The simplest way to gain an understanding of these different forms of concentration is to experience them. The following exercise enables you to explore the different dimensions of attention, and the switching of concentration which you will experience is explained afterwards in fig. 6.2.

Exploring the different dimensions of concentration

Find a colour magazine or book containing a sporting picture and sit comfortably, resting it on your legs with your hands supporting it in an upright position. Ask someone to read these instructions to you clearly and slowly.

1   Study the picture closely. Notice the size, shape, colour and texture of all the objects visible in the picture. While

staring at the picture, mentally list all the features you can see. Try to keep them all in your head at once. Now select a specific object which grabs your attention and stare intently at it. Spend some time studying this object.

2   Now, while you are still looking at the picture, shift your attention to the feeling in your legs where the magazine is resting on them. Feel the weight of the magazine and how easily your legs are supporting it. Keep looking at the picture but notice the feeling in your fingers as you hold it upright. Grip the magazine more firmly and feel the pressure in your fingers increase.

3   Now, while still looking at the picture, imagine yourself in sporting action achieving a glorious victory. Decide which tactics brought you success, and spend some time reviewing yourself in action.

4   Now return your attention to what you can see in front of you. Keep your eyes on the picture but try to notice everything around you in the whole of your visual field. Try to be aware of everything at once.

5   Now focus on the picture once more and look closely at the object which held your attention earlier. Notice every detail you can about that object until it is the only thing you can see and everything else has faded.

6   Now let that object fade from your attention too and slowly return to full awareness of your surroundings.

What you should notice about this exercise is that although your visual field did not change at all, the objects and thoughts to which you were giving your attention varied enormously. As fig. 6.2 shows, you were initially concentrating on the picture in front of you, with your attention directed externally and narrowed on to a specific object. Next you became aware of specific internal feelings in your legs and fingers. This was not a 'loss' of concentration but rather a voluntary switch of attention from a narrow external focus to a narrow internal focus.

As you began daydreaming about achieving a sporting victory, your attention was still fixed internally (this time on your thoughts rather than on your bodily feelings) but had broadened

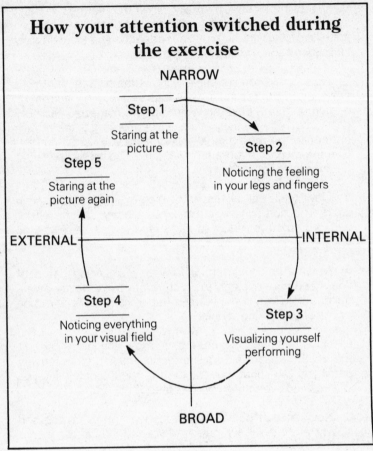

How your attention switched during the exercise

NARROW

Step 1
Staring at the picture

Step 2
Noticing the feeling in your legs and fingers

Step 5
Staring at the picture again

EXTERNAL ———————— INTERNAL

Step 4
Noticing everything in your visual field

Step 3
Visualizing yourself performing

BROAD

Fig 6.2

to consider many factors at once. In other words, you had switched to a broad internal focus. You then returned your attention to external objects and tried to observe many different things simultaneously. Here, you had switched to a broad external focus. Eventually you narrowed your focus once more to a single external object, thereby returning to your original narrow external focus.

As you can see, concentration processes are quite complex and it is not helpful to view concentration as something which simply comes and goes. The process of controlling the direction, width and selectively of attention lies at the very heart of all skilled action, and is particularly vital in sports performance.

A critical fact to bear in mind is that for every type of sports skill there is one type of concentration focus which will aid performance and there are others which will prove detrimental to performance. For instance, if you are taking a penalty flick in hockey and, at the precise moment when you should be focused totally on the ball you are thinking about previously missed efforts, then you greatly increase the chances of missing again. This is because the actual flick of the ball requires a narrow external focus rather than a broad internal one. The following tables list some specific uses in sport for the four types of concentration focus and some of the typical errors of concentration focus.

Typical uses for the different types of concentration focus

Concentration focus	Uses in sport
Broad-external	'Reading' situations Finding a team mate to pass to Noticing the position of opponents Anticipating the action
Narrow-external	Focusing on a specific object, such as a ball, just prior to catching or striking it Focusing on a target when taking aim
Broad-internal	Analysing how the contest is going Deciding tactics Learning and recalling set plays
Narrow-internal	Noticing small details of technique

Being aware of weight
transference and other
small aspects of bodily
movement
Recognizing tension in the
body

Typical errors of concentration focus

Problem	Error
Failure to notice an opponent Failure to notice a team mate in a good position Missing important performance-related details	External focus too narrow
Failure to focus on the ball or target Making simple errors, mis-hits, etc. Seeing details which are unimportant	External focus too broad
Over-analysing situations Not playing the game in the here and now, i.e. going over the past in your mind or anticipating the future Being indecisive	Inappropriate broad internal focus
Saying negative things to yourself Becoming fixed on a particular thought or feeling and missing important things going on around you Worrying about a recent mistake	Inappropriate narrow internal focus

In the last exercise, you explored the different dimensions of concentration, and you probably found that focusing your attention in one dimension was considerably easier than in others. It is quite natural for a particular individual to feel more at home with one type of concentration than with any other. In fact, the preference for either paying close attention to detail or to scanning our surroundings, giving attention to this and that as the fancy takes us, is part of our personalities. In the same way, some people are great thinkers who analyse situations on a grand scale, while others focus closely on particular thoughts and feelings.

Although at any one time the style of concentration we adopt will be determined primarily by the situations in which we find ourselves, it is worth remembering that underlying all switches in attention is a deep-rooted preference for one particular style of concentration. Furthermore, not only is this preference unlikely to change, but at times, particularly during stressful moments in sport, there will be a strong tendency to revert to our own particular style of concentration, whether it is appropriate to the situation or not. This frequently leads athletes to make very basic errors, the sort of mistakes which, quite rightly, are blamed on poor concentration.

INDIVIDUAL DIFFERENCES IN CONCENTRATION STRATEGIES

Certain names in sport have become synonymous with intense concentration: Bjorn Borg, Ivan Lendl, Jack Nicklaus, Steve Davis and Geoffrey Boycott. You can probably think of many more. Concentration, for them, is a relentless process, as though they become detached from their surroundings during performance and occupy their own special worlds.

Other equally successful performers, such as Jimmy Connors, Lee Trevino, Ian Botham and Eric Bristow all seem to be much more a part of their surroundings, interacting with their audience, displaying emotion, but still managing to concentrate when it really matters. The underlying explanation for these differences may be a matter of introversion versus extroversion, but, equally, they can be viewed as alternative concentration strategies.

The intense, solitary approach of a Borg or a Boycott relies heavily on a narrow focus; they attend to selected important details and ignore everything else for long periods of time. It is a very disciplined form of concentration, one that most athletes find too demanding. The more carefree approach of a Botham or a Bristow is in sharp contrast but has proven no less effective. It allows for much 'to-ing and fro-ing', looking around during breaks in the action, perhaps sharing a joke with another performer, occasionally getting lost in thought. This approach relies less on the total exclusion of all distractions and more on the ability to refocus on important precise details as and when required.

What both approaches to concentration have in common is the need for effective control. Make no mistake, when the moment to perform arrives, all great sporting heroes, even those with the most cavalier of styles, are able to focus attention totally on the relevant, the whole relevant, and nothing but the relevant. It is easy for lesser mortals to mistake such versatility for casualness, and fail to appreciate that this control over their concentration represents a truly advanced sporting skill.

Of these two fundamentally different approaches to concentration, probably one strikes you as more natural than the other. My advice to most performers is to develop the skill of refocusing attention at will rather than attempting to harness attention for the complete duration of a contest. Ultimately, it is this ability to banish distractions and produce a clear, uncluttered view of all the relevant details which is the key to effective concentration.

HOW TO DEVELOP CONTROL OVER CONCENTRATION

There may be moments in sport when you are convinced that you are your own worst enemy. Distractions and negative thoughts about your performance may cause you to question just whose side your brain is on. This answer is that, in fact, it is on two sides. That is, there are two sides to the brain and they often appear to be working in conflict.

It is well established that the brain has two separate hemi-spheres which are responsible for different functions. The right side of the brain controls our visual and creative skills, and is essentially the *performer* in us. The left side is the logical, analytical part of us, essentially the *thinker* and the *talker*.

Unfortunately the left side of the brain often inhibits the right side to the point where it can no longer function effectively. Because sport relies heavily on vision and often demands great creativity, the right side needs freedom to express itself. If the talking, analytical hemisphere dominates during performance the flowing improvization which typifies the champion is swamped. Unless stopped, the left side of the brain will constantly dictate what needs to be done and will sit remorselessly in judgement of every action.

This 'Battle of the Hemispheres' can result in action restricted by thought, where an internal focus upon logic and analysis clouds vision and causes tension. In order to prevent this 'paralysis by analysis', where the thinker restricts the performer, attention must be focused visually and, for the most part, externally.

The next exercise shows how to practise maintaining a visual image while excluding analytical thought. This exercise helps to develop the sort of discipline over concentration which will greatly benefit performance. Remember, though, that this control is a skill which requires much practice in order to withstand the pressure of competition.

Holding an image

This exercise, which you can modify to suit your particular sport, develops the skill of maintaining concentration on a specific object for extended periods. You will need a stopwatch for this exercise.

- Find a comfortable chair in a place where you will not be distracted or disturbed. Sit upright, feet flat on the floor, with the stopwatch in one hand and both hands resting in your lap

- Spend a short time relaxing using the five breath technique (see page 124)

- Visualize a yellow tennis ball on a green background, or whatever other image is appropriate to your sport. Notice every detail about the ball, imagine its texture, its size and its roundness. Notice any writing on the ball, and the contrast of the white seams on the yellow ball

- Once you have the image in your head start the stop-watch and try to maintain a clear image for as long as possible. If the image fades or your attention is drawn to any distracting thoughts or sounds, stop the watch. At first you will probably find this very difficult and may stop the watch after only a few seconds. Don't be alarmed if this is the case and above all don't succumb to the temptation to cheat. With practice you will gradually maintain concentration for longer and longer periods

- After each attempt note down the length of time you maintained uninterrupted concentration on the image. Use the principles outlined in the Performance enhancement programme (see page 48) to set goals for each attempt and to monitor your progress. Once you have mastered one image (i.e. you are able to hold the image undistracted for one minute) change to another image which is important to your sport. Alternatively, you may choose to focus on a real object by fixing your vision and your thoughts on it. Stop the watch if either begins to stray.

Once you have learned to restrain the thinker within you, you will begin to trust the performer to do its job unsupervised. As a simple demonstration of just how superior the performer is over the thinker when it comes to physical action, lie down on the floor, flat on your back, and try to explain to yourself the procedure for standing up.

Analyse the required movements, and only move limbs as and when instructed to do so by your logical hemisphere. 'Bend the right leg at the knee until your right foot is flat on the ground,' 'Lift your right arm and move it across your body, placing it palm down on the floor by your left elbow,' and so on. If frustration does not get the better of you, eventually you will figure out the necessary movements. Your performance will, however, be a poor imitation of the highly efficient way you would normally get up.

THE HERE AND NOW

The response which seems to have become compulsory for all soccer managers when asked about the future prospects for their team is, 'We're taking each game as it comes'. This may be a cliché but it nevertheless sums up much that is sensible about performance strategies. It emphasizes the wisdom of focusing on what is happening now and the foolishness of anticipating the future.

Although no sensible person would dispute the need for advance planning in sport and a regular review of tactics, at the precise moment when skills are being executed, attention should be focused on that moment and that moment alone. Timothy Gallwey, of the Inner Game movement, refers to this as being in the 'here and now', focusing attention on all the important details of the present moment and ignoring completely what may happen in the future or what has happened in the past.

The importance of doing this is a vital lesson for all performers to learn. The past is gone and cannot be changed, the future is uncertain but depends on what you do at the present moment. The fact is that when you review past events or get 'ahead of yourself' you just do not attend so well to your current situation. If attention is directed totally towards the here and now the result will take care of itself, but anything which pulls attention away to another time or to irrelevant details threatens the success of the outcome.

For example, the squash player who dwells on the last kill shot he put into the tin is very likely to make further mistakes because he has become preoccupied with the past. Attention divided between where the ball is now and where it was hit before is often enough to tip the balance towards another error.

Remember that the only thing which can be controlled is your behaviour now. You cannot control your behaviour in the past or the future, nor your opponent's behaviour at any time, so learn to live and play for the moment. Sports performance, like life, is comprised of an endless series of present moments. The more of them you are able to control, the better you will play, the more consistently you will perform and the less frustrated you will become with the past, and the less uncertainty the future will hold for you.

HOW CHANGES IN EMOTIONAL STATE AFFECT CONCENTRATION

All skilled action depends for its success, either directly or indirectly, on the way we feel during performance. Superior performances tend to be associated with emotional states such as happiness, contentment and confidence, whereas poor performance is often linked with feelings of depression and anxiety. The way emotion affects physical functioning is by influencing mental processes such as attention.

It has been well established through scientific research that changes in emotional arousal are closely connected to changes in concentration focus. During the course of a normal day, levels of emotional arousal might vary from deep sleep to complete panic and similarly, during the span of a single contest, arousal levels often vary considerably.

The effect of emotional change on the processes of attention can be dramatic. As sport tends to heighten the emotional state of its participants, when a problem occurs it is usually one of over-arousal. The effects of over-arousal on attention can be summarized as follows:

- An increased reliance on the preferred style of concentration, whether it is appropriate to the situation or not

- Loss of control in switching from one type of concentration focus to another

- A tendency to over-analyse, with attention shifting from external details to an internal focus

- Involuntary narrowing of attention towards a particular object, thought or feeling, for example, getting a particular thought 'stuck' in your head.

Each of these effects is a potential threat to performance. The scale of the problem can be judged by analysing the typical response to a simple mistake, such as a golfer missing a short putt or a tennis player crashing an easy volley into the net. The initial error itself usually results from poor concentration but, to

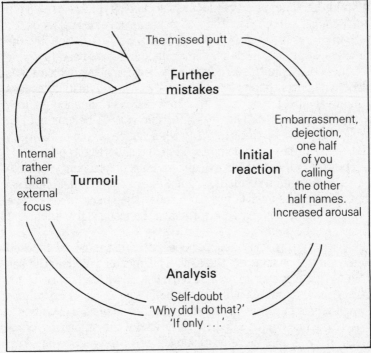

Fig 6.3

compound the problem, the mental confusion which follows often destroys all semblance of composure and sends arousal levels rocketing. The order of events is often as shown in fig. 6.3:

All mistakes are followed by an initial emotional reaction, usually a mixture of dejection and anger, which is very often accompanied by name calling, where one half of you chastises the other half for its stupidity. The self-recrimination usually continues silently as the mistake is replayed and analysed in the mind, planting the seeds of self-doubt. As the action proceeds, the inner conversation often continues, with the memory of the last mistake sitting on your shoulder like a demon, forbidding you to do it again.

'You missed the last putt but don't miss this one.'
'Don't you dare miss this one.'
'You simply cannot miss this putt.'
'Oh God, you missed this one as well.' (Screams and bellows)

The original error magnifies and reproduces itself because

attention becomes internally focused, locked on your own thoughts and feelings, when in fact the skill demands an external focus.

Sometimes this vicious circle, often set in motion by the simplest of errors, ends up damaging self-esteem and lowering confidence. Again this is due to excessive analysis which takes place when attention is fixed internally. When a mistake causes emotional upset it is easy to allow self-recrimination to lose perspective, so that 'That was a terrible volley', becomes 'I just can't volley', which turns into 'My whole game is going to pieces', and, in some cases, to 'I suppose I'm just a worthless person'.

The fact is that this form of analysis has no place in a sporting contest. Attention divided between external action and internal thoughts results in an ill-prepared and rushed performance. The more thoughts dominate performance the less clearly important details will be seen.

Once strategy has been decided, attention must be focused totally on the business of the skill. This means watching the ball intently and tracking its path through the air with laser precision. The golfer, Tony Jacklin, described this as 'a state where everything is pure, vividly clear . . . a cocoon of concentration'.

A technique which is particularly useful for stabilizing emotional arousal and thereby making control over concentration easier, is referred to as 'centering'.

Controlling emotional arousal by 'centering'

This technique is known as centering because it involves focusing attention on the centre of the body, the area just behind your navel. This has a calming and controlling effect, providing a simple but effective way to counteract over-arousal. It is best to practise centering in a standing rather than a sitting position because, during a contest, there probably will not be a seat available. The procedure for centering is as follows:

- Stand with feet flat on the ground, shoulder width apart, arms hanging loosely either side of the body

- Close your eyes and breathe evenly. Notice that when you breathe in, the tension in your upper body increases, but as you breathe out there is a calmer, sinking feeling

- Inhale deeply from your abdomen and, as you do, be aware of the tension in your face, and your neck, and your shoulders, and your chest. As you exhale, let the tension fall away and focus on the feeling of heaviness in your stomach

- Continue to breathe evenly, focusing all your attention internally on the area immediately behind your navel

- Maintain your attention on that spot and breathe normally feeling very controlled and heavy and calm.

During moments of extreme emotion, this simple technique allows you to regain a feeling of relaxation and control very quickly. With sufficient practice this can be a matter of only a few seconds. It might help if you quantify how heavy you feel at any moment by selecting a number between one and ten which best represents your state of heaviness, where one is extremely light and ten is extremely heavy. In time you will learn to recognize your ideal level of arousal and should become able to 'breathe' yourself up or down to the number which represents that optimum level.

You can demonstrate the effectiveness of centering to yourself with a little experiment. Find two volunteers of about the same size and weight as yourself and stand between them. Bend your arms at the elbows and brace yourself so that you feel immovable. Ask them to lift you by pushing up underneath one elbow each. They will probably lift you quite easily.

Now try the same thing but 'centre' yourself first. Make sure your assistants allow you sufficient time to centre, but do not warn you of when they will be lifting. If you have centred effectively your state of relaxation will make you much more difficult, if not impossible, to lift.

The technique of centering will enable you to prevent changes in emotional state from interfering with concentration, but you will need to recognize when you are under- or over-aroused. During practice, get into the habit of identifying situations which tend to make you tense up and others where you find yourself a little too relaxed. By doing this you will be able to predict the times when centering will help.

This chapter has dealt with the dangers of attention divided between the job at hand and irrelevant thoughts or distractions.

Hopefully by now you have a better understanding of what good concentration means and how you can achieve it. I must re-emphasize that you will need to work at these control skills, but also that the practice will be worth it. Here are the key points to remember:

- Think about the demands of your sport on your concentration and decide *where* your attention should be and *when*

- Learn to restrict self-analysis during performance

- Learn how to narrow attention effectively, and how to fix attention on specific objects

- Don't allow increased arousal to interfere with control over attention.

This discipline is often the final frontier for performers. Unfortunately, years of frustration and missed opportunities may pass before you fully appreciate and begin to come to grips with the problem. Ask yourself how long you want to wait before you become the master of your powers of concentration. The solution is in your hands.

A PROGRAMME FOR TOTAL PREPARATION

By now you will probably have thought a great deal about the mental side of performance. You may well have already started implementing some of the mental skills exercises as a regular part of your training programme. You are possibly still a little unsure of the best way to fit it all together to make prime use of your valuable training time. This final chapter is designed to help you slot everything into place to create a programme which will prepare you totally for competition.

Efficient preparation is all about choosing the right priorities, and that means making clear decisions about where to concentrate your efforts. At the very beginning of this book, I proposed that performance depends upon your level of skill, your physical preparation and your psychological readiness. On a pie chart, that formula might look like the ones in exercise 12.

The relative importance attached to the three slices of the performance pie will vary greatly from person to person. Logically, the overall shape of your training programme should be a reflection of the way you view the performance demands of your sport. So ask yourself, how big a slice of performance do you believe is determined by your mental approach, by your skill level and by your fitness?

All athletes and coaches have their own opinions. Gus D'Amato, the late manager and trainer of boxer Floyd Patterson and the adoptive father of current World Heavyweight champion, Mike Tyson, always maintained that 'fights are won and lost in the head'. Tyson's total concentration and ferocious intensity are no doubt a reflection of D'Amato's influence.

Each factor in the performance pie is vital in its own way and each should therefore have its place in the training schedule of a

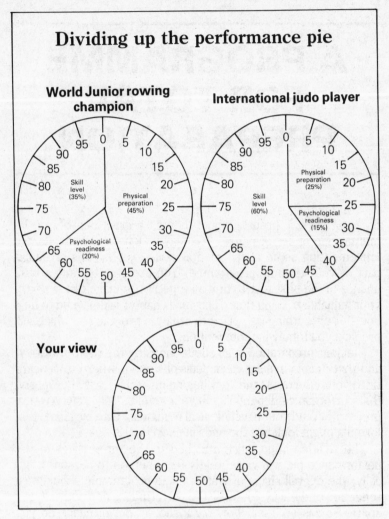

Dividing up the performance pie

World Junior rowing champion

Skill level (35%)
Physical preparation (45%)
Psychological readiness (20%)

International judo player

Physical preparation (25%)
Skill level (60%)
Psychological readiness (15%)

Your view

Exercise 12

competitor. Physical skills and tactical awareness form the basis of your ability to perform; physical fitness forms the basis of your ability to last the course; and a tough mental attitude which enables you to stay confident, handle pressure, and maintain concentration forms the basis of your ability to win consistently.

In exercise 12, divide up the performance pie for your sport as you see it by quantifying the relative importance of skill, physical preparation and psychological readiness. To give you some idea

Mike Tyson

what other athletes think, two examples from the world of rowing and judo are included. When you have finished this exercise, review your actual training schedule in the training schedule exercise.

Now compare your training pie with the performance pie for your sport. Does your training accurately reflect what you believe to be the performance demands of your sport? Does the amount of mental skills training you do match the importance you attach to psychological readiness? If not, the implications are obvious.

SCHEDULING MENTAL SKILLS SESSIONS

The next step in your programme is to set aside realistic practice periods every week to allow the mental skills to develop. Fig 7.1 shows the general outline of a training week, which reflects an assessment of the performance demands in the sport of triple

Analysing your training schedule

1   How many hours per week in total do you train?

_____ hours

2   How many hours are devoted primarily to fitness?

_____ hours

3   How many hours are devoted primarily to skills work?

_____ hours

4   How many hours are devoted primarily to mental skills?

_____ hours

Divide the answer to the second question by the answer to the first question and multiply by 100. This represents the percentage of total training time devoted to fitness. For example, if you spend a total of 12 hours per week training and three of those hours are devoted primarily to fitness, then 25 per cent of your training emphasis is on fitness. Do the same for questions three and four.

5   Percentage of total training time devoted to fitness?

Question 2 ÷ question 1 × 100 = _____ %

6   Percentage of total training time devoted to skills work?

Question 3 ÷ question 1 × 100 = _____ %

7   Percentage of total training time devoted to mental skills?

Question 4 ÷ question 1 × 100 = _____ %

Now enter these percentages on your training pie.

Exercise 13

Your training pie

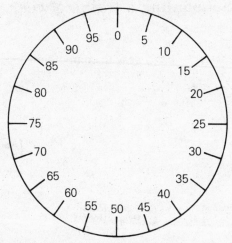

jumping. Remember that a training schedule is best established in collaboration with your coach.

The athlete in Fig. 7.1, who is a seasoned international competitor, presently views performance as 45 per cent skill, 30 per cent physical preparation, and 25 per cent psychological readiness. His training schedule reflects this exactly. Of the ten hours per week spent training, four-and-a-half hours are devoted to technical work, three hours to fitness and two-and-a-half hours to mental skills.

At different times during the training year, or indeed at different times during the athlete's career, his or her perception of the performance demands might change and this should be reflected in the training schedule. For example, during the winter months between competition seasons, when the foundations of fitness are laid, the emphasis would be on heavy physical work, but as important competitions approach, the emphasis would move to the technical and mental aspects of the sport.

The points to remember when scheduling your training week are:

- Balance physical work with mental skills to avoid excessive fatigue

- Avoid physical work when ill or injured

- Do not commit yourself to a schedule you cannot fulfil

Scheduling a training week

Sport: Triple jump
Training period: Early season competition

	Mon	Tues	Wed	Thur	Fri	Sat	Sun
08.00							
09.00							
10.00						↑ Mental practice ↓ (30 mins)	
11.00							
12.00							↑ Fitness (Sprints) (1hr)
01.00	↑ Concentration control ↓ (15mins)	↑ Centering (15mins)	↑ Concentration control ↓ (15mins)	↑ Centering (15mins)			Technical (1½hrs) ↓
02.00							
03.00						↑ C	
04.00						O M P	
05.00						E T I T	
06.00						I O N	
07.00	↑ Technical (1½ hrs)	↑ Fitness (weights) (1hr)	↑ Technical (1½hrs)	↑ Fitness (weights) (1hr)		↓	
08.00							
09.00							
10.00	↑ Relaxation (20mins)		↑ Relaxation (20mins)		↑ Relaxation (20mins)		
11.00							

Training week summarized:

Technical work   3 × 1.5 hours
              TOTAL = 4.5 hours

Fitness work   3 × 1 hour
              TOTAL = 3 hours

Mental skills   3 × 20 mins
              4 × 15 mins
              1 × 30 mins
              TOTAL = 2.5 hours

Fig. 7.1

- Be specific about when and where you are training.

PLANNING THE MENTAL SKILLS PROGRAMME

Once the commitment to a mental skills programme is made, the programme should be planned to give you the maximum return on your investment of time and effort. A format which has proven to be effective for a vast range of sportsmen and women follows a clear pattern where, after some form of self-assessment, each mental skill is developed thoroughly and this is followed by an evaluation of the skill's effectiveness when used in competition. This process can be summarized as:

**Assessment . . . Education . . .
Implementation . . . Evaluation**

Assessment phase

Having a clear awareness of your playing strengths and weaknesses acts as a springboard for self-improvement. This is as true of your mental approach to competition as it is of your physical skills. A thorough review of your psychological characteristics give a mental skills programme the necessary direction.

After working your way through the exercises in this book you will have a heightened awareness of your psychological strengths and weaknesses. If you haven't done so by now, make sure that you assess all of the following personal characteristics in the space given in exercise 14:

- Your ability to use visualization
- Your personal need for achievement and fear of failure
- Your susceptibility to anxiety
- Your personal images of confidence
- Your strengths and weaknesses in concentration.

Psychological profile
(example)

Name: *Martin Dickson*   Event: *Triathlon*

Visualization ability (*Ring the appropriate number*)

	V. Poor				Average				V. Good		
Sight	0	1	2	3	4	5	6	7	(8)	9	10
Sound	0	1	2	3	4	5	6	(7)	8	9	10
Feel	0	1	2	3	(4)	5	6	7	8	9	10
Smell	0	1	2	3	4	(5)	6	7	8	9	10
Taste	0	1	2	(3)	4	5	6	7	8	9	10

Comments: *Need to develop greater vividness when visualizing. Must create a greater feel for movement. Practise twice a day.*

Motivation levels

Need for achievement

0　1　2　3　4　5　6　7　8　(9)　10

Fear of failure

0　1　2　3　4　5　6　(7)　8　9　10

Comments: *Must recognize that losing is not failure. Set goals related to technical development and effort rather than winning.*

Images of confidence

Required performance qualities
1. *Aggression*
2. *Determination*
3. *Control*

Positive self-statement

A shark in the water, smooth on the bike, tunnel vision during the run.

Exercise 14

Concentration characteristics

Key performance details   Major distractions

1. Focus on the man in front (swim)
2. Transition routine
3. Rhythm during cycling

1. Own thoughts
2. Concern for others
3. Memory of previous defeats

Strengths in concentration
1. Good at sticking to race plan
2. Good at deciding tactics
3. Usually very focused at the start.

Weaknesses in concentration
1. Tend to get distracted as race progresses
2. Mind wanders during cycle phase
3. Too judgemental in pressure situations

Anxiety characteristics

Situations which provoke anxiety:
1. Facing an opponent with a big reputation
2. Being kept waiting at the start
3. Not having a toilet available at the start
4.
5.

Strategies for coping:
1. Positive imagery, emphasize strengths
2. Relaxation techniques
3. Replanning routine
4.
5.

Comments: Develop a pre-competition routine allowing time for the loo and including
relaxation and positive imagery.

Psychological profile

Name: _____　　Event: _____

Visualization ability (*Ring the appropriate number*)

	V. Poor				Average				V. Good	
Sight	0	1	2	3	4	5	6	7	8	9	10
Sound	0	1	2	3	4	5	6	7	8	9	10
Feel	0	1	2	3	4	5	6	7	8	9	10
Smell	0	1	2	3	4	5	6	7	8	9	10
Taste	0	1	2	3	4	5	6	7	8	9	10

Comments: _____
_____
_____

Motivation levels

Need for achievement

0　1　2　3　4　5　6　7　8　9　10

Fear of failure

0　1　2　3　4　5　6　7　8　9　10

Comments: _____
_____
_____

Images of confidence

Required performance qualities:–

1.
2.
3.

Positive self-statement:–

1.

Concentration characteristics

Key performance details:–   Major distractions:–
   1.   1.
   2.   2.
   3.   3.

Strengths in concentration
   1.
   2.
   3.

Weaknesses in concentration
   1.
   2.
   3.

Anxiety characteristics

Situations which provoke anxiety:
   1.
   2.
   3.
   4.
   5.

Strategies for coping:
   1.
   2.
   3.
   4.
   5.

Comments: _____
_____
_____

Exercise 14

This self-assessment will be of most benefit if it is all put together to form a complete psychological profile of yourself. In turn, this profile should form part of a complete performance diary in which you record every detail of your progress. You can design the performance diary to suit your particular needs. Exercise 13 will have given you some ideas of what the psychological profile should contain.

One area of psychological assessment which has not yet been completed is the identification and recognition of your ideal performance state. In the last chapter we discussed how performance is affected by your level of physiological arousal, which should be at its optimum level just prior to and during competition.

Identifying your personal optimum arousal level can prove more difficult than you might imagine. Memory is notoriously unreliable in highly charged situations and, although many athletes feel that they perform best when relaxed, often such judgements are based upon nothing more than vague recollections. Some performers become anxious, even alarmed, when they notice symptoms of high excitement and they aren't really sure whether these high levels of arousal actually hinder or enhance their performance.

It is impossible to accurately prejudge the level of calmness or excitement that is ideal for any particular individual. Certainly a great number of athletes *are* at their best when very relaxed, but many others perform better when excited or even agitated. Every athlete would be well advised to use a systematic approach to help them identify not only at what level of arousal they perform at their peak but also to learn how to recognize the bodily responses which signal when they are at just the right level.

Exercise 15 provides you with a checklist of arousal and anxiety symptoms, and a means of recording excitement levels in relation to performance levels. If you complete this exercise over a series of 10 to 20 competitions, a pattern is certain to emerge. You will begin to notice a connection between the quality of your performance and how excited you were just before the start. Your ideal level of excitement is that which regularly coincides with your best performances.

Recognizing that you are not at your ideal performance level and actually doing something about it are not the same thing, but clearly one precedes the other. If you have followed the exercises in this book you should be proficient at lowering your

Identifying your ideal arousal level

Complete this exercise several times just prior to the start of competitions. If on any occasion this proves impossible, then fill in the details shortly after the competition has finished while they are still fresh in your mind.

Date: _____ Competition: _____

1 Rate the importance of this event

    0   1   2   3   4   5   6   7   8   9   10

Not important at all   Average importance   Vitally important

2 Rate how excited you feel at the moment

    0   1   2   3   4   5   6   7   8   9   10

Sleepy Lethargic Bored   Extremely excited

3 Tick which of the following you are experiencing at the moment or have experienced in the last few minutes

Pounding heart	____	Butterflies	____
Rapid breathing	____	Clammy hands	____
Dry mouth	____	Need to visit toilet	____
Tight neck/shoulders	____	Trembling	____
Distorted vision	____	Yawning a lot	____
Nausea or vomiting	____	Feeling weak/heavy	____
Fear	____	Irritability	____
Lightheadedness	____	Voice distortion	____

Complete this part after competition

4 Rate how well you performed

    0   1   2   3   4   5   6   7   8   9   10

Terrible   Excellent

5 What was the competition result?
_____

Comments: _____
_____
_____

Exercise 15

arousal level using either a simple relaxation technique (see Five breath technique on page 124) or a Concentration control technique (see Centering on page 144).

If, on the other hand, you find it necessary to heighten your arousal level this can be achieved in a variety of ways, ranging from explosive aggressive movements to positive self-talk. The world's strongest man, Jon-Pall Sigmersson, uses a great Viking roar to psych himself up and Geoff Capes slaps himself on the face. The table summarizes a variety of ways to manipulate arousal, some to get you 'up' when arousal needs heightening, and others to calm you down if you begin to lose control.

Uppers

1 **Self-talk**
   Simple phrases such as 'I'm excited' can help channel fear into positive arousal. Also, repeatedly saying 'I'm ready' to yourself in a vigorous tone can heighten arousal level.

2 **Rhythmic chanting**
   A technique favoured by African tribes and soccer crowds. Chanting any phrase over and over again, even something as simple as 'Here we go, here we go, here we go', can lead to a collective fervour in group situations.

3 **Shouting**
   With both of the previous techniques, heightened arousal is promoted partly by increased volume. In fact, shouting is both a symptom and a cause of rising emotion, as anyone who gets involved in heated arguments will testify.

4 **Physical contact**
   Rugby players frequently pound themselves (or one another) with their fists in order to get 'fired up' before a match, and providing physical injury can be avoided, gentle forms of abuse are effective methods of lifting passions.

5 **Physical exertion**
   Vigorous activity, especially where all-out effort is required, will increase arousal. Therefore, sprinting (on the

spot will do), fast press ups or squat thrusts could be used. However, because most sports involve a great deal of physical exertion, the activity itself will tend to push arousal up which is why techniques for lowering arousal frequently become necessary.

Downers

1 **Relaxation**
Depending on the circumstances available, any one of the techniques outlined in chapter 5 will be effective in controlling over arousal.

2 **Positive visualization**
Visualizing yourself performing successfully in competition, or mentally recreating your 'winning feeling' or invoking your personal images of confidence, will all help to calm you prior to a contest.

3 **Distraction**
If the prospect of competition causes too high a level of anticipatory excitement, then switching attention to a more mundane task, such as moving equipment around, is a simple solution which 'takes your mind off' the future.

4 **Mental rehearsal**
This method of control is equally effective before a contest or during a break in the action. Focusing attention exclusively on one skill and running it through in the mind brings about a feeling of calmness and control.

5 **Centering**
This technique (described on page 144) is designed to reduce arousal levels by focusing attention on a particular point within the body, where your centre of gravity is located, and 'breathing' your arousal down. Again this method can be used before or during performance.

Education phase
The education phase of the programme is simply the period allotted to learning the mental skills which contribute to your

winning mentality. It is difficult to prescribe the amount of
practice which should be allocated to each skill. You may master
some of the skills in a week, others may take you a year or
more. There is general tendency, however, for athletes to
cease practising before they have actually mastered the skill
completely. For instance, it is common for an athlete to practise a relaxation technique a few times under conditions which
are not stressful, and then to think 'Yes, I've cracked that one',
only to find that, in competition, the ability to relax deserts
him.

It has been emphasized many times that mental skills are the
same as physical skills in the sense that they both take hours and
hours of practice under increasingly realistic conditions before
they will stand up to the intense pressure of competition. There
are no short cuts to success in sport and all education programmes demand diligence and patience. Unfortunately, count-
less athletes push themselves through harsh physical training
regimes only for their minds to prove the weak link in
competition.

A mental skills programme is no magic wand but in the long run
it may make the difference between winning and losing. However, it must be approached realistically. Ensure that you
schedule adequate time periods to develop each mental skill in
turn and above all be patient with yourself. The mental skills
explained in this book are unlikely to give a dramatic boost to
performance immediately, but given time they will help you
control and release the full power of your potential.

Implementation phase

The education phase of the programme is the mental equivalent
of all the physical skills work you undertake. By the same token,
the implementation phase closely parallels those periods of
strategic thinking when tactics are decided upon and a gameplan
is formulated. Preparing totally for competition involves planning
for every conceivable eventuality, and shoring up the performance weaknesses that become evident.

To do this thoroughly you should refer back to previous
exercises in the book. For instance, the Routeplanner exercise
(see page 42) can be used to decide the basic strategy for
improvement. Exercise 16 shows a fairly typical plan for implementing a mental skills programme to overcome a common

Planning the implementation phase

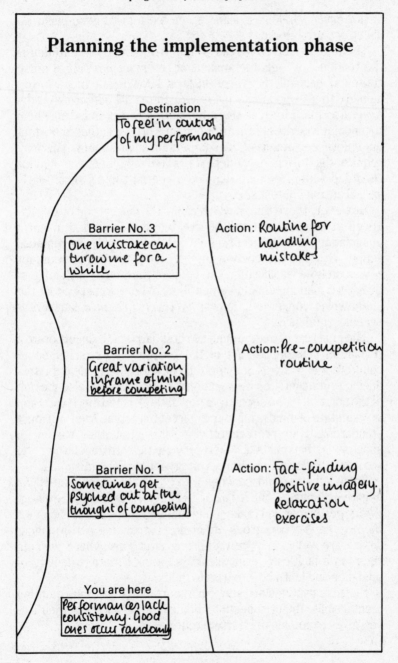

Destination

To feel in control of my performance

Barrier No. 3

One mistake can throw me for a while

Action: Routine for handling mistakes

Barrier No. 2

Great variation in frame of mind before competing

Action: Pre-competition routine

Barrier No. 1

Sometimes get psyched out at the thought of competing

Action: Fact-finding Positive imagery. Relaxation exercises

You are here

Performances lack consistency. Good ones occur randomly

Exercise 16

performance weakness; namely, the feeling that good performances occur randomly.

The first perceived barrier to improvement for this athlete is the tendency to become anxious at the mere *prospect* of some contests, particularly where little is known (but much is imagined) about opponents or venue. Remedial action may take several forms. Firstly, a thorough fact-finding exercise may help to pinpoint weaknesses in an opponent's play or gather important but unforeseen details of the competition environment. This may require the coach or athlete to watch opponents in live or recorded action, or may demand a special trip to, or an early arrival at, the contest site.

However, those things which cannot be discovered or experienced in advance can still be created and controlled in one's imagination, and this represents the second step in remedial action. Review the section on preparing for competition for advice on how visualization can be used to remove any sense of threat from an impending competition. Where anxiety about the unknown is concerned, familiarity (even *imagined* familiarity) breeds confidence.

The final part of overcoming the first barrier is to incorporate a relaxation session as part of the precompetition schedule to counteract any lingering symptoms of worry. This idea of introducing routine into the preparation for competition is also the hub of the solution to the second barrier. If there is too much variation in your state of mind prior to the start of the action, then you must standardize your preparation. Similarly, if another barrier to success is that mistakes disrupt your performance, then the answer is to devise a routine strategy for handling mistakes.

Some athletes and coaches view 'mistake management' as negative thinking, but it is not negative, it is simply realistic. Every performer will make mistakes, and there is no reason for them to have a disastrous effect on your overall performance. There are very, very few sporting situations where winning requires a faultless performance, so accept the inevitability of mistakes and learn how to handle them.

Because routines are such an important part of implementing mental skills, the next section outlines the principles of their use and gives examples of effective routines.

COMPETITION ROUTINES

Consistent outcome results from consistency in your physical routine and your concentration routine. Routines are equally useful both to prepare you for competition and at pre-determined moments during competition. As most sportspeople are creatures of habit, it is quite likely that you already follow some vague routine on the day of a competition. Therefore, it should be quite an easy job to develop this into a detailed precompetition plan which will give you the feeling of being in control and of being totally prepared for competition. These feelings are often at the heart of an athlete's confidence.

Preparing for a competition

There is no single all-embracing preparation which is ideal for everyone, but for each individual there is an ideal routine which suits their own personal needs. It will be up to you to identify the precise routine which puts you in the correct frame of mind to compete at your best, but these guidelines and the example should help you.

Guidelines for competition routines

Competition routines should be:

- **Controllable** Wherever possible design a routine which relies upon no one other than yourself. Being let down by someone just before you compete can have a devastating effect upon performance

- **Positive** Know what you are going to do rather than what you are not going to do. For example, it is better to make the decision to 'complete a 15-minute stretching routine half an hour before the contest starts' rather than just saying 'I will not sit around worrying in the changing room'

- **Personal** Remember that the ultimate test of a competition routine is not what other people think about it but whether it helps you. All athletes have their own set of unique likes and dislikes and only you can decide what routine is effective

- **Detailed** Make sure that your routines are specific enough to be reproduced time after time. As a general principle, they should be more detailed as competition time approaches.

An example of a precompetition routine for a triple jumper

Behaviour	Comments	Countdown to performance
Wake up	Smile. Say, 'Today's the day'	7.45 on the morning of the competition
Eat a leisurely breakfast	Cereal, toast and honey, coffee. Say, 'I feel good.'	8.00
Shave/shower		8.30
Get dressed	Shoes, not trainers. Smart, confident	8.45
Check kit: Spikes, insoles, pants, 2 pairs socks, shorts, vest, tee-shirts, track-suit, rain-suit, walkman, tapes, food, money, trainers towel, soap, shampoo, chequebook	Remember spike key and new spikes.	9.00

Behaviour	Comments	Countdown to performance
Leave for competition	Have one final look in the mirror. Say, 'I look the business.' Spring in stride. Buy newspaper	9·15
On journey	Sit down as much as possible. Listen to music, read paper.	
Confirm time of event with coach.		
Mental rehearsal of warm-up and jumps	Slow and thorough	4 hours
Eat lunch	High in carbohydrate	3 hours
Arrive at venue. Look at track layout, check pit, board distance, runway, bounce	'I'm here and it feels good.'	1½ hours
Get changed, go to toilet		1¼ hours
Begin warm-up – 800m jog, stretching routine	Methodical progression through body	50 mins

The winning mind

Behaviour	Comments	Countdown to performance
Striding/bouncing. Full speed, measure run up and mark	Pick up tempo. Think 'power' and 'floating'.	30 mins
Practice run-throughs	Focus on technique	10 mins
Report in. Check order and position.		5 mins
Sit down. Mental rehearsal of first jump	Think 'power' and 'floating'.	2 mins
Stand up. Vigorous stretching, pumping actions	Think 'pump up', get excited.	1 min
Get ready as previous jumper begins. Tee-shirt off, then bottoms. Touch toes, double-footed vertical spring.	Get angry, emotional. 'Come on, now!'	30 secs
Foot on marker, head up, eyes fixed.	Wait for wind to drop.	10 secs
Visualize jump then GO!	See a big one	0 secs

Fig. 7.2

During a competition

There are frequent moments during a competition which call for
absolute control and composure. The last minute penalty, the six
foot putt on the 18th green, the final service game to win the
championship. These can all be heart-stopping moments. When
the contest comes to the crunch, it is very easy for the mind to
focus on the consequences of actions rather than their performance. Nothing is more likely to cause composure to evaporate
than allowing attention to wander in this way. The same tendency
to review what should have happened or could have happened
often occurs following mistakes, and has disruptive consequences.

The way to prevent this from happening is to develop competition routines which become such well rehearsed rituals that
nothing disrupts them. Sandy Lyle preparing to putt, Ivan Lendl
preparing to serve, even, to some extent, Eddie Edwards
preparing to launch himself down the 90 metre ski jump, all have
familiar and very consistent routines. The more winning and
losing hangs in the balance the more crucial these routines
become.

Competition routines should include a physical ritual which
precedes key skills *and* a mental checklist. In fact, of the two, the
mental checklist which controls your concentration focus is the
more important. The secret of successful competition routines is
that they are precise and well rehearsed. The next examples
demonstrate the sorts of routines which are effective.

People sometimes dismiss routine as the gaoler of natural flair.
They feel that routines encourage predictability. Well, up to a
point they do. They make peak performance more predictable
and spontaneous lapses less likely. Remember that flair does not
emanate from chaos, it involves choosing the correct, but somehow unexpected, option. Flair demands the coolest head in the
most heated moment. It rides on waves of confidence which in
turn are fed by the feelings of personal control which routines
induce.

Evaluation phase

The evaluation of any programme tends to take place on several
levels. Invariably you will make some form of intuitive evaluation
of anything you do, and hopefully once your mental skills programme is under way, you will gain the general impression that it
is beneficial. More than this though, you will quite naturally look
to performance as an indicator of whether the programme is

An example of a competition routine for an Olympic épée fencer

Purpose: <u>Recovering composure</u>

Behaviour	Self-talk
Move away from the opponent. (Physically distance myself from the mistake.)	
Correct the mistake in my mind. (Straighten blade if necessary.)	'Use your acceleration'
Use centering to regain control.	
Return to 'en guard'	
Focus attention on a single aspect of technique	'Lead with tip'

Fig. 7.3

An example of a competition routine for a Junior International tennis player

Purpose: <u>Preparing to serve</u>

Behaviour	Self-talk
Decide where serve is going.	
Foot to line	
Relax physically (center)	'Controlled power'
Visualize the serve	
Focus the target area	Think 'smooth'
Serve	

Fig. 7.4

worthwhile, particularly whether you are winning more often than you were before. This is understandable, but as the sole indicator of success, a win-loss record is misleading. My advice would be to evaluate your efforts systematically but on a broader basis than victories and defeats.

Refer back to the Performance enhancement programme on page 48 for the general strategy which will enable you to evaluate the programme fairly. Throughout this book I have been advocating the principle that gradual but sustained progress is the route to ultimate glory, and therefore the true test of any programme, be it skills, fitness or mental training, is whether improvement is taking place. The establishment and monitoring of short-term, intermediate and long-term goals provides the best mechanism for judging the effectiveness of your mental skills programme. Accordingly, accurate and detailed records of your progress will need to be kept.

A mental skills training diary is an effective way of monitoring progress for several reasons. It encourages you to be thorough in your preparation, it records in black and white improvement which may otherwise be overlooked, and it allows for detailed planning based on what has been effective in the past. The time you invest in keeping it up to date will be repaid many times over.

There is a great volume of books about sport, many written by Olympic and world champions, several of which recall how the great achieved their greatness. Naturally, there is much to learn about winning from those books. The unique aspect of this book is that it sets out to help you discover for yourself exactly why and how your mind helps you to win or keeps you from winning.

The book has offered a short cut to techniques which many champions discover instinctively during long competitive careers, but which innumerable other athletes never fully come to grips with and so greatness always eludes them. Neither this book nor any other can promise you greatness, but what it will have given you is a very great boost in your quest for fulfilled potential.

FURTHER READING

PSYCHOLOGICAL SKILLS (GENERAL)

Albinson, J. G. & Bull, S. J. (1988) *A mental game plan: A training program for all sports*. Available from: Sports Dynamics, 49 Twickenham Rd, Teddington, Middx TW11 8AH.

Carron, A. V. (1984) *Motivation: Implications for coaching and teaching*. Available from: Sports Dynamics, 49 Twickenham Rd, Teddington, Middx TW11 8AH.

Harris, D. V. & Harris, B. L. (1984) *The Athlete's guide to sport psychology: Mental skills for physical people*. Available from: Eddington Hook, 406 Vale Rd, Tonbridge, Kent TN9 1XR.

Railo, W. (1986) *Willing to win*. Available from: Eddington Hook, 406 Vale Rd, Tonbridge, Kent TN9 1XR.

Syer, J. & Connolly, C. (1984) *Sporting body, sporting mind*. Eddington Hook, 406 Vale Rd, Tonbridge, Kent TN9 1XR.

PSYCHOLOGICAL SKILLS (SPORT SPECIFIC)

Gallwey, W. T. (1986) *The inner game of golf* Pan.

Gallwey, W. T. (1986) *The inner game of tennis* Pan.

Sacks, M. H. (Ed.) (1984) *Psychology of running*. Eddington Hook, 406 Vale Rd, Tonbridge, Kent TN9 1XR.

Unestahl, L. E. (1983) *The mental aspects of gymnastics*. Available from: Orebro, Sweden: VEJE Publ. Inc.

FITNESS (GENERAL)

Anderson, B. (1980) *Stretching* Pelham.

Hazeldine, R. (1985) *Fitness for sport* Crowood Press.

Murray, A. & Lear, J. (1983) *Power training for sport* Batsford.

Ottoway, P. & Hargin, K. (1985) *Food for sport: A handbook of sports nutrition.* Resource Publications.

Peronnet, F., Thibault, G., Ledoux, M., & Brisson, G. (1987) *Performance in endurance events* Available from: Sports Dynamics, 49 Twickenham Rd, Teddington, Middx TW11 8AH.

Radcliffe, J. & Farentinos, B. S. & R. C. (1985) *Plyometrics: Explosive power training* Available from: Eddington Hook, 406 Vale Rd, Tonbridge, Kent TN9 1XR.

Read, M. & Wade, P. (1984) *Sports injuries: A unique guide to self-diagnosis and rehabilitation.* Breslich & Foss.

Sharkey, B. J. (1984) *Physiology of fitness.* Available from: Eddington Hook, 406 Vale Rd, Tonbridge, Kent TN9 1XR.

Tancred, B. & Tancred, G. (1984) *Weight training for sport.* Hodder & Stoughton.

FITNESS (SPORT SPECIFIC)

Hawkey, P. (1984) *Fit for squash* Batsford.

Juba, K. (1988) *Fit for swimming* Pavilion.

Meade, R. (1984) *Fit for riding* Batsford.

Palmer, S. (1986) *Fit for alpine skiing* Stan Palmer.

Risman, A. B. W. (1984) *Fit for rugby* Batsford.

Risman, A. B. W. (1986) *Fit for tennis* Batsford.

Stirling, J. (1984) *Fit for golf* Batsford.

Woodland, L. (1988) *Fit for cycling* Pavilion.

Yaxley, J. (1986) *Fit for soccer* Batsford.

INDEX